POWER
OVER
POWER

POWER
OVER
POWER

What power means in ordinary life,
how it is related to acting freely,
and what it can contribute to a
renovated ethics of education

DAVID NYBERG

Cornell University Press

ITHACA AND LONDON

Copyright © 1981 by Cornell University Press

All rights reserved. Except for brief quotations in a review, this book, or parts thereof, must not be reproduced in any form without permission in writing from the publisher. For information address Cornell University Press, 124 Roberts Place, Ithaca, New York 14850.

First published 1981 by Cornell University Press.
Published in the United Kingdom by Cornell University Press Ltd., Ely House, 37 Dover Street, London W1X 4HQ

International Standard Book Number 0–8014–1414–8
Library of Congress Catalog Card Number 81-67053
Printed in the United States of America
Librarians: Library of Congress cataloging information appears on the last page of the book.

For Noah's mother, my love

Contents

Preface

From time to time I like to tease my students with the following syllogism:

> If Francis Bacon was right in saying that "knowledge is power," and
> If Lord Acton was right in saying that "power tends to corrupt and absolute power corrupts absolutely,"
> Then we must conclude that "knowledge tends to corrupt and wisdom corrupts absolutely."

As is the case with most teasing, this kind gets serious after a while. The logic of the syllogism is sound but its conclusion is disturbing and apparently false. The problem must be in the premises: Bacon, Acton, or both may be wrong. On the other hand, each could be right in what he claims, but have a different concept of "power." In that case the meaning of the argument depends on the ambiguity of its key term—power—and the equivocal use of that term accounts for the syllogism's puzzling implication. In fact, the concept of power *is* ambiguous, and its relation to knowledge and corruption, or more broadly to education and ethics, is far from clear.

The question of what power has to do with education and ethics is perhaps one of the most serious issues that confront any civilized society. A preliminary investigation into the literature that has accumulated around this question led me to two interesting discoveries. First, beginning with Thucydides, Socrates, and Plato, the idea of power has attracted the attention of many philosophical thinkers, and since Machiavelli it has prompted an uneasy concern in the social sciences. Yet in spite of this chronologically extended and logically intensive consideration, power remains troublesome, its meaning almost enigmatic, its ethical status confounding. There remain a deep conceptual ambivalence in the literature about power and an uncomfortable psychological ambivalence in its readers. My second discovery is that there is no serious and sustained analysis of power itself in the literature of education. When power is mentioned, and it frequently is, it is used without definition or analysis, as if we already had a clear grasp of its meaning. It is not unusual to see "power" in the title of a book on education, but then, because the concept is not discussed at all within, we are unable to find it in the index.

The discovery that power theory remains inconclusive and that power has been literally expurgated from educational studies provided the incentive for this book. What follows is an account of my inquiry into the concept of power, the forms it takes in ordinary life, how it suggests new ways to think out problems of freedom, and how it helps to give us a fresh perspective on some educational questions that the tired arguments of garrulous commentators have led us to ignore far too long.

My inquiry has been an adventuresome hunt for new ideas, the kind of hunt that is necessary for preserving an interest in thinking, but that risks being incomplete, oversimple, and either "too philosophical" (that is, not enough data) or "not philosophical enough" (that is, logically unpersuasive). I accept these risks and offer this book as an invitation to the debate over what power means, whether and how its practice should be taught, and what place that practice has in contemporary ethics and education. Like good dialogue on other important ideas, this one may be endless and consensus may elude us. But the life of the mind is enriched by the very activity of rethinking what we do not fully understand, and by the attempt to harmonize lyricism and analysis in the process.

I am grateful to many good friends whose generous gifts of thoughtful criticism, guidance, and encouragement have enriched this book. The influence of David Bazelon's thinking about power is apparent throughout Chapter 2; I learned much from him in many hours of challenging conversation and in the class we taught together at Buffalo in 1978. In that class, and since, Robert Dischner, Michele Twomey, and John Ramsay compelled me to reconsider what I was trying to teach them about power. Stephen Brown, Kieran Egan, Jon Emerson, Maxine Greene, Hugh Petrie, Jonas Soltis, Jack Thomas, and Lawrence G. Thomas—these are friends whom I regard almost as partners in my work because they have given me so much to think about and have shown me, by their own examples, better ways to think (although I'm sure not all of them would find this book to be evidence that their influence has been successful).

No author could be more pleased than I with excellent editors; Barbara L. Burnham and John G. Ackerman of Cornell University Press deserve my deeply realized gratitude for all they have done. My very special secretary, Eileen Raines, with help from Marilyn DelNagro and Nancy Myers, typed the manuscript through several drafts, always with careful skill. Thanks are due also to Robert Dischner and Paul Farber for preparing the index. Nancy Nyberg has given me far too much to reckon here—my feeling is reflected in the dedication.

DAVID NYBERG

Buffalo, New York

POWER
OVER
POWER

Introduction: Rethinking
the Obvious

In this book I scrutinize two aspects of ordinary life in America and meditate a renovation of educational philosophy. My premises are simple. First: power is a fundamental category of all human experience, but it is badly misunderstood and often taken to be an immoral characteristic belonging to those who oppose (or ignore) the various forms of Judaeo-Christian ethics. Second: freedom is one of the most frequently used, most important, and most ambiguous words in English, but there is no existing logic of freedom which helps to explain freedom's ambiguity and show how it might be taught as a practical value. Third: both knowledge of power and the practical skills of freedom can and should be taught as the ethical minima for getting on as decent people in contemporary western society, but this is not now the view of any philosophy of education. Fourth: given that power and its distribution, freedom and its practical existence, and educational plans are all critically important to democratic government, each deserves a sustained and critical rethinking.

This rethinking is meant to rejuvenate debate on serious issues that are so much with us in everything we do that they tend, like too much strong sun, to be taken for granted, to make us drowsy and reluctant to face them directly. I want to break habits and to make problems in our assessment of power, freedom, and education; to bear down on what people actually do when they grapple with power, when they want to act freely, and when they seek to provide (an) ethically sound and useful education for the young. To get at the substance of the problems, it is necessary to pay attention to the language we use to describe, and frequently to disguise, our actions. It is especially important to clarify the language of power in relation to freedom and education, for power has become something of a bad word in our culture—a word not often talked about and almost never analyzed in relation to educational processes, purposes, and policies.

Such neglect is a dreadful mistake, for *power is unavoidable in all social relations that involve at least two people related through a plan for action.* Power is a part of everybody's daily life. It concerns not just the rich and greedy, the armed and forceful, the elected (or appointed) and official; but everybody. A pious antipathy to the subject is the sort of denial that eventually leads to anomic suicide, Bedlam, or Nuremberg. Less dramatically, one may say that this refusal to recognize the pervasiveness of power breeds a sense of powerlessness and default, the effect of which is to concentrate power among the few who are willing to understand it. In trying to break our cultural habit of willful ignorance about power, I am working for its wider distribution. Power tends to concentrate most narrowly when knowledge about it is not widely shared. The distribution of knowledge about power, then, is a necessary protection for democracy's basic design.

Yet we are a people of extreme ambivalence about power. We want it in general as a nation but fear it in particular as it appears in groups and individuals. We are beside ourselves on the subject. ("Paranoia" comes from the Greek *para,* beside, and *nous,* self.) Many intuit a connection between power and organization—and indeed there is one—but then fail to study the implications. Instead, by simple association, organizations become phobic foci, like the power they incorporate. Some of us go so far as to see power and organization as necessarily ene-

mies of freedom, objects that humane education ought to overcome. Such thinking is profoundly wrong and shows how
drastically we must rethink the central terms of our discussion. Power, freedom, and education are related terms that
describe interdependent aspects of any civilized social community; we must recognize that all three are essential to the
fulfillment of our democratic aspirations in both public and
private life.

I might even say that the most important questions that we
face in social science and political philosophy are the questions
of the relations between freedom and organization, between
power and organization, and therefore between freedom and
power. We must begin a renovation of these conceptual categories and attempt to establish an ethics for an education
that teaches knowledge about power and the skills of freedom.
In this book I want to lift the black hood from power and the
gossamer veil from freedom, making both accessible to the
influence of reason. I want to make each of them teachable
and to argue that they ought to be taught.

Power Talk

For our own good, we must learn how to talk about power,
and to participate effectively in the various power relations
in which we inevitably find ourselves (as parents, spouses, employees, employers, citizens, voters, consumers, group members, and neighbors). We must talk about power without resorting to idiotic euphemisms and insipid rationalizations for
what we do and what we fail to do.

At the same time we must learn to speak sensibly of freedom,
first by recognizing that there is no general problem of freedom. We must accustom ourselves to thinking in terms of particular persons who want to realize some specific aim within a
particular set of circumstantial constraints. As things stand,
the idea of freedom has lost its edge, it has been so dulled
through generalization that it is useless as a thinking tool.

Much talk of freedom actually inhibits thought because the concept has come to stand for a categorical good without anybody knowing what it means. Power, on the other hand, is commonly, but not always, treated as categorically bad—especially when it is associated with people other than ourselves and our friends.

I would argue that this desire to make freedom Good and power Bad without knowing what either one means is evidence of a larger desire for the absolute, for some form of totalism. This yearning is one of the most destructive of human passions. It fosters a language of ultimacy which cannot be the language of the commonplace, of compromise, patience, tolerance, practicable analysis, and liberal dispute. In short, it cannot be the language of ordinary human life, or the language of this book.

Language is both the record and the instrument of change. We must guard important words from the deadening effects of carelessness and overuse—we must try to keep them from becoming clichés that no longer serve any purpose in the activity of reasoning about important problems. As words harden into cliché, ideas are reduced to platitudes. Sometimes it seems that our success in providing a little education for a lot of people has brought on a plague of platitudes as one of the curses of modern culture. The remedy, if there is one, must be a mixture of analysis and lyricism, but as Freud found out, such medicine may be too strong for the fainthearted. Freud's critics were not used to his language and demanded to know why, for goodness sake, all that talk about sex was necessary. They wondered why he couldn't use more genteel words like intimacy, love, and affection. No, Freud responded: "I like to avoid concessions to faintheartedness. One can never tell where that road may lead one; one gives way first in words, and then little by little in substance too."[1] He was talking about sex and he did not want to lose sight of that; he was afraid of being sidetracked from the bedroom to the parlor by the sweet smell of euphemism.

Why my insistence on *power* talk? Couldn't I restate my

points on the manifestations of power in everyday life by using such terms as influence, effectiveness, charisma, leadership, authority, and leaving power to describe those "other people"? The problem is that such a concession would prevent thought on power from developing beyond its present state, and expurgate power from educational philosophy altogether. This expurgation of power is exactly the conceptual error that I am trying to avoid.

In a survey of more than thirty encyclopedias, dictionaries, and handbooks in special fields (political science, philosophy, sociology, social psychology, psychiatry, education, management, religion, and law), the most interesting fact I discovered was that about two-thirds of them do not even contain an entry for power.[2] One of these works, *The Encyclopedia of Human Behavior,* has an introduction that states that the volumes' purpose is "to present essential information on surely what is the most important subject of all: man's knowledge of himself." Power does not appear as an aspect of this "essential information."

In some of those works that do attempt to define power, the entries are too vague to be of much help (e.g., "A behavioral dimension defined as ability to satisfy needs . . . or to prevent their satisfaction"[3]), and several others were steeply slanted normative judgments, like the two below:

[Power is] the ability or authority to dominate men, to coerce and control them, obtain their obedience, interfere with their freedom, and compel their actions in particular ways.[4]

The threat of force is the basis of some forms of power, but more genteel and prevalent forms of power depend on deception and deceit. Power of the latter type does not resort to brute force, but rather to the manipulation of the morality of others for the selfish ends of the person wielding this type of power.[5]

Such red-faced moralizing does not help to clarify matters. There are a few entries that do help to clarify what power means, notably those by S. I. Benn (*The Encyclopedia of Philosophy*, VI, 424–27), R. A. Dahl (*International Encyclopedia of the Social Sciences*, XII, 405–15), and B. H. Raven (*International Encyclopedia of Psychiatry, Psychology, Psychoanalysis, and Neurology*, IX, 7–11). Benn is helpful in pointing up problems with power as a relation between people, and he examines the place of intention and influence in power theory. Dahl's essay sets out a list of descriptive and explanatory characteristics that aid in classifying types of political power. Raven identifies six bases of social power which help organize the social psychological research on power in groups. These three articles establish an objective framework for considering power in philosophical, political, and psychological terms.

The conclusion I draw from the survey is that although power is used widely as a descriptive concept, there is little if any agreement about how to use it as an instrument for thought. Power will not disappear but so far it has not been clearly identified, either. Nothing in the extensive literature of power stands out more clearly than the fact that power is perceived to be part of life itself—and just as stubbornly resists satisfactory definition.

The Fetish of Freedom

Although not much has been written on the concept of power in a context of educational philosophy since Plato's *Gorgias*, the situation is very different when one turns to freedom. Education and freedom are so intertwined in American thinking that it is difficult to mention one without referring sooner or later to the other. If Americans are ambivalent and somewhat paranoid about power, they have made a fetish of freedom, endowing it with the magical power to save its possessor from harm. It is an object of devotion.

Freedom has been used constantly, if not consistently, as a challenge to dogmatism, and, as such, it appears in talk of education more frequently than almost any other term. Still, as

W. J. McCallister wrote in 1931, "no adequate presentation of [freedom's] essential meaning for practical schemes of education has hitherto been undertaken."[6] His observation remains valid today, in spite of *Summerhill,* open education, and the politics of desegregation. After all, a fetish takes part of its charm from ambiguity.

Ideas of freedom, like those of education, are conditioned by the cultures and traditions of which they are a part. Given the diversity of cultures and traditions in a persistently pluralist society, one would not expect a single and convincing answer to the question of freedom's meaning for education to be forthcoming, despite the unanimously positive regard for freedom as an ideal. Nevertheless, we engage ourselves with the idea of freedom, as with other great themes, hoping at least to "enlarge and fortify the mind," to borrow a phrase from Rousseau, who gave us one grand enigma on the subject in his *Émile.*

Freedom seeks to challenge fate and social influences, to devise an answer to force, and to control passion, in order that human beings can produce intentional effects in this world. In this sense, I view freedom as the rational operation by which people devise, and implement plans. Freedom is the possibility that follows our assumption that things do not have to be as they are. It is the idea that people can challenge God, Nature, and Society for control over what happens. It is chutzpah. It is a luxury. And most important of all, when understood as a set of learnable, teachable skills, freedom has compelling practical consequences for schemes of education. Simultaneously, freedom loses its mystique, its talismanic qualities, and takes on the worldly character of a craftsman's trade.

But this understanding is difficult to achieve in a society that encourages people to "want freedom as spontaneously and directly as babies want milk."[7] Such an understanding requires a shift of sentiment and perspective from the view that freedom is "natural," wonderful, and an ultimate end, to the view that it is a rational achievement that requires constant work, implies responsibilities, and is of instrumental value only as a means to other ends. In this respect freedom is much like power and, indeed, the two concepts have much in common and stand in close relation to one another by virtue of their similar psychological, social, and instrumental attributes. Both depend on an individual's plan or intention, and both are best thought of as means to chosen ends, rather than as ends in themselves.

Education Overload

There is no doubt that near universal exposure to some amount of education and the culture of higher education has produced a change in sensibilities. We are now basically a nation of half-educated people, certainly not yet even half a nation of educated people, and this is a significant achievement with serious implications for the future of power and freedom in America. One often overlooked, underestimated consequence of education is an increase in dissatisfaction with the way things are. If there is any truth to the homily that ignorance is bliss, then education is the corruption of contentment. By exposing a mind to the possibility of *possibility,* to the rudiments of "as if" thinking and the world beyond personal and present experience, educators create the conditions of discontent. In blunt terms, unhappiness is the consequence of many kinds of learning and, as a result, education is politically important.

A truth of politics is that politicians cannot afford to have the voters mad at them. An educated and well-informed constituency can be big trouble; a half-educated constituency can be big trouble, too. The ignorant and still mind is easier led than the informed and active one. A little learning is a dangerous thing, from a political point of view, because it produces discontent— often with the politicians themselves. Discontent among the constituency must be taken into account, and because it is so important it acts as a control over politics. Public education that goes beyond mere socialization is thus a source of chagrin to the less democratically inclined, and this is one reason that America will always need it. Jefferson apparently had this situation in mind when he warned us that any nation expecting to be both ignorant and free expects what never was and never will be. And so he argued that *some* public education was essential to democracy itself.

Given the fears of the politicians, there is a delicious irony in the fact that the thing educators think they cannot afford is to have their constituency mad at them. Pleasing that various constituency seems to be the truth of contemporary education, and the result is a bit of a consternation for all concerned. Some fear that in trying to do too much, education actually does too little. Others, focusing their attention on the amorphous and touchy area of "moral education," fear that education will be successful in doing what it has no business doing. The first group points to what it considers a surprising and disgraceful decline in tested achievement among students through the secondary level, and the deplorable state of literacy in the country as a whole. The latter group is indignant over the schools' pretensions to form the character and conscience of its children, especially when the schools present a model for character and conscience that parents do not think fit either for themselves or for their children.

The attempt to cater to everyone who has a claim to a "free public education" thus produces education overload. Education is trying to be too much for too many.[8] Two contemporary social values are the ultimate sources of this overload: activist pluralism and sentimental moralism.

Pluralism is group politics as contrasted with party or class politics. Against strong odds, pluralism has survived the schools' early and sustained efforts at culture mulching— "Americanizing," or "acculturation." People today identify themselves socially and politically through all sorts of groups and category affiliations (e.g., sex, ethnicity, age, occupation, religion, education, and any combination of single issues such as abortion, affirmative action, the ERA, environmentalism, capital punishment, Israel), and they form a political network of complex coalitional interactions which is always changing and hard to read.

Educational institutions try to maintain a display of programs that will satisfy all the claims placed upon them—claims for both open and traditional classroom styles; for sports programs that transcend sex differences and academic programs that suit the special needs of all kinds of special students; for enrollment statistics that emphatically do not reflect the ethnic compositions of established neighborhoods and for some surviving trace of local community influence on policy; for a guaranteed minimum competence in basic subjects and for at least the possibility of excellence in something chosen by individual students; for exploration and for more discipline, and so on. The complete list would make one despair at the hopeless ambition that overloads American education with policies, purposes, and programs. This is not to say that the pluralist motive behind this situation ought to be jettisoned for some other. Pluralism is as close to a traditional cultural value as we have; it should be conserved, and it should be used to inform our ethics of education. But it should not dominate reason and overshadow all other motives in constructing educational programs.

I think we should face the fact that schools are not good for much, and they never have been. Rather than make them responsible for more than was ever reasonably conceived as their responsibility, we should try to force the issue back in the other direction: toward making schools very good at meeting fewer responsibilities by concentrating on what they are good for.

To consider such a reversal in emphasis seriously, one must first recognize the sentimental moralism that is the source of much of our thinking about education. This is the morality of "get-well" cards, expressing the all-purpose Hallmark hug and hope that things will be better soon. In facing choices between claims on class time, one is reduced figuratively to picking a card—it doesn't much matter which, because they all say approximately the same thing. No one should be denied an "appropriate" but noncomittal greeting. Denial would be rude, for it would violate the basic premise of this morality which is that this sentimental gesture, however meaningless it may be, shall be equally distributed.

Such a view perpetuates the illusion of a "real self" that is somehow better than the aggregate of multiple selves we present from day to day. It promises the eventual actualization of this more authentic self once the right psychological conditions, including an intense introspection, prevail. The battle is the same as that which Rousseau imagined between the sweet homunculus within and the sour social-political-institutional oppression without. It is the real self versus the real world, *ipso facto*. It is the psychology of sentimental egoism.

The most troublesome aspect of this sentimental psychology is neither its evangelical excess, nor its artificial isolation of individuals from social transactions and organizational contexts, but its proclivity to oversimplification. The very idea of one real self represents the psychological antithesis of political pluralism. The latter is a social system that constantly reorganizes, reconstitutes, and redefines its "personality." There is no "real society"—all the coalitions are real, as are all the temporary societies they constitute. In comparison, the quest for the one real self is reductionist. Its favorite colors are black and white, it prefers "me" to "us," and it abhors the constraints of organization—all of which means that it will never help us understand either power or freedom. Both power and freedom are inherently social concepts, but sentimental moralism is not—even though it does try to erase the difference between private and public through openness in self-expression.

The problem of education overload should be approached by reconsidering the two values, pluralism and moralism, which contribute so much to it. Pluralism must be conserved as a genuine American tradition, but educational policy and the scope of educational programs should not be expected to treat the whole horde of implications which follows. While continuing the honorable and generous behavior toward interest groups which is the obligation of a pluralist society, we must recognize that public institutions and social agencies in addition to the schools must assume responsibility for much of that obligation. As educators try to make hard choices about what is basic and indispensable for school curricula, they will not be helped by sentimental moralism and its reductionist egalitarianism. These choices must be made soon, and this book is offered as a step toward making them.

Part I /

THE PROBLEM
OF POWER

There are two main emphases in this book—the recasting of power as an essential concept in social life, and the recasting of freedom as a corollary, rather than as a polarity of power.

Part I deals with power, first as a concept that arouses ambiguous feelings and has produced many conflicting theories. In Chapter 2 the essential characteristics of power are sorted out and synthesized into a new configuration. Finally, the four forms of this configuration of power are named and illustrated.

1 /

The Prominent Ambivalence of Power in America

Power talk excites attention in most circumstances; it is not a neutral subject. We are sensitive to talk of power in a way that suggests our profound fascination with the very idea, a captivation charged with deep feeling and frustrated by superficial understanding.

Two factors help to explain this sensitivity to power. First, all members of all social groups, starting with the family, have had personal (and probably traumatic) experience with power and powerlessness. No social being can escape experience with power and powerlessness, and for this reason power should be recognized as a fundamental category of human experience. People sense the ineluctability of power in social relations and attend anxiously to its presence because its threats and promises determine most of their social intercourse. The second factor to keep in mind is that people only rarely discuss power openly. Straight talk about power is thus something of an event; it is like talk of sex and death for children whose curiosity has been tantalized by adult reticence.

When power does become a direct topic of conversation, the discussion usually focuses on other people's power, not one's own. Most such talk is also complaint about tyrannical, portentous, elitist, usurped, or undeserved power. This pejorative slant strengthens the impression that power is not fit for polite conversation, that an interest in power talk must itself be suspect, and that talk of power sullies the speaker and may corrupt or alarm the chary listener, much as carnal talk is reputed to have done in the Victorian parlor. In short, power is something of a difficult, indelicate topic and a dirty word.

But if power is both an unavoidable part of social life and a dirty word, it should be no surprise that the human mind is sensitive to talk of it and is fascinated with the prospect of satisfying its keen interest with an equally keen understanding. The conflict between the facts of social experience and the irrational interdictions placed on certain words that describe those facts produces an appreciable psychological tension. This is the tension of taboo, a cognitive double take that signals both importance and denial. If one wants to understand power, it will not do to make it a taboo subject or to deny the tension it causes in social life. This kind of "moral" reluctance to confront the power aspects of personal behavior and social relations has prevented adequate investigation of power as a concept germane to all social analysis.

This almost paradoxical condition of power signals its fundamental importance and suggests to me a comparison with the paradoxical condition of sex which Freud confronted in analyzing individual neuroses. His therapy consisted largely in helping patients talk about their repressed experiences by lifting the interdictions of sexual taboo.

American ambivalence about power is in large part the consequence of contradictory teachings that leave one both wanting and fearing power. On one hand, the theme of achievement, which holds a prominent place in American culture, is taught to the very young as a positive expression of power, as the ability to become what we invent or imagine for ourselves. We are taught to strive for and take pride in achievement, and to respect the achievements of others. The magnitude of one's achievement is the measure of this positive power. On the other hand, Americans reject the European tradition of authority in all its monarchic regalia, maintaining that there is no higher human authority than the free and independent individual, and that rule without popular consent cannot be legitimate. Until recently, some families still manifested the regimen of monarchy, but for the most part this last vestige of the old authority is vanishing, replaced by the ideal of consent. In replacing that tradition, consent stands as the central principle of the American idea of freedom.

We have somehow associated achievement with a positive and authority with a negative sense of power, dropping the word itself from talk of achievement while emphasizing it in talk of authority, especially that kind of authority which interferes with individual wants. It is true, however, that social psychologists have gone to great lengths in constructing an "achievement motive" and correlating it with various aspects of character and development, and they go even further in describing an "achieving society" as typically American.[1] This emphasis on achievement is kin to the profit motive and capitalism (and the idea of a meritocracy) in its emphasis on individual effort as the proper determinant of status within the (work) organization. The concept of achievement has a partly egalitarian character because work is meant to supplant privilege in the distribution of income and other resources; but as a normative principle the competitive achievement motive helps to legitimate the ultimate inequality in the distribution of those resources.

There is something good about being ambitious, tenacious, and even aggressive in achieving a planned intention. Indeed, some have become so enthralled with the smell of achievement that they regard it as a basic human need. But there is something clearly bad in the uneven concentration of power which results when resources and status are hoarded by a successful few. The sweet smell of success, to the unsuccessful, turns sour, and power becomes rank (in both senses).

Americans want power as individual achievement and fear it as organizational control. Power educes anger as well as fear when it is perceived in others (the very rich, for example) or in things (weapons) that threaten to destroy the artifacts and natural circumstances of one's self-interest and self-protection. Following the lead of the social psychologists, we come to suspect that a "power motive"[2] drives others secretly to amass and conceal the wherewithal to destroy us. But we calm ourselves with the statistical insight that we all have this power motive to one degree or another, and since it is dangerous only when it gets out of hand, we must simply be alert to signs of unusual interest in power, which are the portents of villainy.

This is the process by which power is cloven from morality; it is the root of our profound ethical ambivalence: we want power because it is necessary for realizing intentions, for achievement; we fear it because it tends to entrench the status and control of others. Power is good because it helps to make order out of chaos; it is bad because it tends to corrupt both character and freedom. Americans like to think of theirs as a powerful nation (bringing order out of chaos), but they resent the powerful individuals and organizations within the nation, feeling that they menace individual freedoms. Given an international context, one is powerful by association as the citizen of a powerful nation, but when individuals compare themselves with their more powerful fellows, a sense of powerlessness is apt to predominate. It is never easy to think about the power of individuals in social relations because doing so confronts one with one's own powerlessness. It is far easier to think of the power of one's country, of one's organization, because organization represents power, and as a part of the organization one is part of the power. The sense of powerlessness of course persists when organizations of which one is not a member are perceived as more powerful.

If it is psychologically stressful to desire what one fears and thinks bad, it is equally stressful to live a life of debilitating powerlessness. Either choice, it seems, is for decadence. This forced (and false) choice, based on a chronic misunderstanding of power, suggests an explanation for the oddly common attraction to submission in American society. Submitting to someone or something else's power (variously called authority, influence, or leadership) is a way to reconcile one's desire for what is fearful and bad with one's aversion to the extreme vulnerabilities of abject powerlessness. The answer is to be close to power[3] but to call it something that sounds more legitimate than power, for example, leadership, charisma, persuasive influence.

America has become a society of groups and organizations. For such a society the question of legitimization becomes crucial because a group's legitimacy affects its ability to organize, and organization is intimately related to the dynamics of power. In America there is a widely shared illusion, one often given official reinforcement by the president's actions, that political and other public activities that require legitimation can be separated from considerations of power and brought under the exclusive influence of moral principles. What makes this humane and otherwise intelligent thought an illusion is not its appeal to moral principles for guidance in political and social affairs, but rather the opposition that it posits between power and morality. This is the same error that was discussed above in more psychological terms. The formulation of a dichotomy between Morality and Power is a conceptual catastrophe, and it almost guarantees that the forces that favor morality in this world will never become powerful enough to contest successfully the forces that favor self-interest. As long as Americans feel repugnance for any sort of power analysis in the social relations that affect them personally; as long as they distrust power per se as an enemy of morality and freedom; and as long as they shrink from admitting the existence of power in everyday social relations—power will continue to concentrate in the hands and organizations of those whose purposes may indeed threaten the moralists who nurture this common illusion.

At the same time, there is no useful category distinction to be drawn between institutions and individuals in discussing a concept so fundamental to social life. All social relations on every scale can be more fully understood if we first recognize and try to comprehend their power dynamics. Power language is thus equally appropriate to the analysis of international relations, corporations, committees, and a single love affair. To deny that the idea of power applies to the understanding of one's personal relations is to perpetrate an intellectual distortion and an ethical charade.

Twenty years ago Dorwin Cartwright pointed out that "twentieth century social psychologists have been 'soft' on power,"[4] that they have evaded serious investigation by studying pecking orders among chickens and children, by reducing power to mere perceptions or attitudes, and by looking at such dubious quantifiables as "prestige" in all sorts of contexts. It was his view then, and I agree now, that "it simply is not possible to deal adequately with data which are clearly social psychological without getting involved with matters of power."[5] Power is inevitably involved with and necessary to the explanation of the major problem areas of social psychology, sociology, political science, education, and other disciplines. Any theory in these areas which does not include a concept of power is incomplete, and because they remain "soft" on power, most such theories *are* incomplete. To say that our theories are so inadequate is not to imply that scholars in these fields (education excepted) have ignored power; the problem is instead our unsettled understanding of power—what it is, how it works, and what forms it takes.

My conception of power is broad enough to cover the world of social relations and organizations, but I explicitly exclude the world of mechanical-physical operations. I have drawn on the writings of many others who have attempted to define the concept and I am much in their debt. The literature on social power is huge, and I cannot pretend to synthesize all of it as a prelude to what follows. But I can give an idea of the range of views that are still in active competition.

Some regard power as a personal motive, trait, or "drive" that becomes part of one's personality, often as the result of an attempt to compensate for some early or repeated experience of weakness or inadequacy. Others believe that power is a special "gift" of vision or charismatic leadership for which there is no adequate, rational account; one is either born with it or without it. Still others see power as a curse of corrupted civilization, its ugly head rising precisely when morality has been abandoned.

Power has been regarded as an end in itself, and as a means to other ends. As a means it is sometimes understood as a subcategory of influence, but influence is sometimes viewed as a subcategory of power. Persuasion is regarded as the opposite of power, though it can also be an example of it, while manipulation is taken to be an aspect of both, of neither, or of power alone.

Some claim that force is the root of all forms of power; others drastically limit its role. Violence has been regarded as the opposite of power and as its very essence. It can be argued that power and authority are inextricably related or that the two are separate and categorically different.

Many maintain that power is an aspect of organization, of status, of position, and not a characteristic of individuals. This can mean that class structure determines all forms of power, but some would insist that this is the work of hierarchy. Some believe that the traditional, economic, or legal bases for sanctioning social behavior are the deep clues to the nature of power. But to some people sanction means coercive intervention as a means of enforcement, while to others it means the exercise of moral authority, or "authorization."

Power is regarded as a controlled exchange of goods and services at all levels of social life, but can it not also be seen as the consequence of the breakdown of such an exchange system? It is spoken of as a possession and as an attribute of certain activities—thus one may or may not "have" it even while one "exercises" it.

In short, many patterns of relation have been proposed to define power, but none has succeeded in attracting consensus among those who have created the literature. If there is a guiding social or political principle behind this book, it is that a broader distribution of power in society is a condition that ought to be pursued, and that pursuit of this condition is contingent on a broader distribution of knowledge about what power is. The concentration of power is protected by a concentration of knowledge about power. Ignorance and powerlessness are related in such a way as to suggest that education has a special place in any future redistribution of power, and that education itself is a powerful social force. The study of power, then, leads to a renovated study of education.

2 /

The Very Idea of Power

In 1887 Lord Acton wrote a severely critical review of Mandell Creighton's *History of the Papacy during the Reformation* and sent a personal letter to the author in which he defended his point that popes and kings ought to be held to account for the criminal acts they authorize. That letter was the context for Acton's mighty maxim: "Power tends to corrupt and absolute power corrupts absolutely."[1] Although it remains the best-known sentence ever written about power, it is only a partial truth.

There are two levels of meaning in Acton's aphorism: (1) that *power* tends to corrupt, and (2) that absolute power (always) *corrupts*. Perhaps the nefarious Nixon White House Staff is a good enough example of the first sense. Its members all gave the impression, and some gave testimony, that they could not resist the corrupting effects of their powerful new positions, and that they were a little surprised at their own debasement.

But what are we to make of someone like the killer who, feeling his personal state to be impotent and wholly lacking in self-respect or the respect of others, chooses to become somebody by killing a well-known person, or a lot of less well-known people? This sort of corruption surely comes from powerlessness and not from power. Rollo May has gathered case studies to support the view that precisely those who do not develop a sense of, or a position of power in the everyday social world are the ones most likely to become corrupted psychologically and morally in ways that lead to violence.[2]

It may well be then that human beings have multiple sources and talents for corruption, but the question remains whether absolute power always *corrupts*. I would challenge the very possibility of *absolute* power, if by absolute we mean "accountable to no one." I argue later that all power is delegated and because of this it is accountable to those whose consent and delegation support the power-holder's position. I will use absolute power to mean "much effective social power." Stalin, Hitler, and Joe McCarthy are clear enough examples that power *corrupts,* but what of other powerful people such as Lincoln, Gandhi, Franklin Roosevelt, and Martin Luther King whose power did not apparently corrupt them? What of a mother's near absolute power over her infant, or of the tutor's power over Rousseau's Émile? It is no good to say that although people like these have wielded great influence and effected enormous social changes they have not used power, or they were not people of power simply because they were not corrupted by their success. Such argument begs the question of how power, in all of its social forms, is related to corruption. It will not do simply to say that if what we took to be power did not actually corrupt, then it must have been something else posing as power (charisma, leadership, influence, or moral authority). Power is power even though it comes in many different forms, is used by many different kinds of people for all sorts of purposes, and is difficult to manage well.

Nevertheless, public suspicion of power per se lends support to Acton's presumption, and his nifty phrasing will continue to mislead people in their thinking about power, especially those who feel they have none themselves and are victims of those who do. Edgar Z. Friedenberg's epigrammatical twist—"All weakness tends to corrupt, and impotence corrupts absolutely"[3]—is amusing and partially true, but it will never defeat the original for mass appeal because most of us, while recognizing that we are (relatively) weak, do not want to think we are corrupt, as well.

The effect of Acton's aphorism has been to simplify our view of a complex concept. For this he is not so much to blame as are those who quote him heedlessly. Power is complex and can be defined only in terms of its various facets. An appreciation of power's complexity makes it possible for one to re-examine its place in ethics.

Facets of Power

My image for the labor of defining the facets of power is that of the lapidary at his stone. Power is the stone, identified by Niccolò Machiavelli half a millennium ago, and like Mephistopheles it was broken away from its place in the coalescence of human psychology and left to develop an independent and infernal character of its own. The banished stone has remained nearly untouched since the quondam Florentine statesman stood before it, the sun at his back for a closer look, and cloaked it with one of the longest shadows in all of Western civilization.

The stone has a rough, hard crust and is believed to possess esoteric evil qualities. (Diamonds were at one time thought poisonous, too.) My lapidary chips at it and, like a sculptor, seeks the forms contained within—forms that he believes are there to be discovered, displayed, and reconciled with ordinary life.

What then does the idea of power mean?[4] Bertrand Russell argued for the importance of the question when he said that "the fundamental concept in social science is Power, in the same sense in which energy is the fundamental concept in physics."[5] He elaborated briefly by asserting that the "laws of social dynamics are laws which can only be stated in terms of power, not in terms of this or that form of power ... power, like energy, must be regarded as passing from any one of its forms into any other, and it should be the business of social science to seek the laws of such transformations."[6] Russell then stipulated his definition of power as "the production of intended effects"[7] and went on to describe various types of power, leaving the search for power transformations to others.

That power is *a* fundamental concept in social science, if not *the* fundamental concept, I take to be a given. To begin with, power is inherent in social life. We cannot choose whether power shall be present as a quality of relations among people; we can only choose whether to think about it, to understand it, and thereby improve our chances of managing it. Whenever at least two people are related in some way relevant to at least one intended action, power is present as a facet of that relationship. The minimum and necessary conditions of power are two people and one plan for action. This means that power is partly psychological and partly social.

Power is never only psychological: it is not merely a property of some minds and not others, nor is it a special individual trait or motive as Winter,[8] McClelland,[9] and psychologists before them have tried to show. It does not make sense to think of a recluse, a hermit in complete isolation, as having power or being powerful, no matter what is in his mind. We say such a person lost what power he had in the very act of retiring from the world of social relations and public notice. Other psychological traits and properties of individual minds such as capricious thought, whimsical moods, and deluding imagination are easy to associate with isolation from other persons; power is not.

But power is never only social either. At least two persons are necessary, and that makes power at least social, but more is implied by the concept. One of the persons must intend an action and have a plan—no matter how inchoate—to do something. The mental activity of the planner involves foresight with some degree of organization and control of information. The mental activity of the other includes some form of consent to the planner or to the plan itself. The relation between the one's intention to act and the other's consent to that intention is close to the heart of power theory. This relation suggests another facet of power, namely, that it always exists in connection with a state of relative powerlessness. One consents to the other, and transfers power with that consent.

In addition to being social and psychological, power is also always instrumental. It is a means; it is not a commodity. The Latin root of power is *posse,* to be able. Power is thus an action idea that exists in the mediation of events and must be judged by its effects. Although always *of* a situation, power can emerge from or precipitate particular events.

Each of these three facets of power needs further explanation.

The Social Aspect of Power: Order Out of Chaos

Chaos, the shapeless, turbid mixture of all potentialities, has been both the genesis of social life and a hazard to human survival. It posed the first metaphysical question, all answers to which were premised on the idea of relation. Chaos contained all seeds of all things, but none in relation to another, and because of this it was everything and nothing; it was intolerable. In chaos there was no pattern to the modes in which one thing stood to another; neither causal nor consanguine connections held things together. In chaos, the metaphor of absolute freedom, thinking itself is impossible because thinking depends on the ordered relation of ideas. Relation is the primordial philosophical idea by which we come to understand all other ideas. There is no good without better and bad, no truth without certainty and doubt, no justice without fairness and inequity, no freedom without independence and enslavement, no reason without faith and ignorance—no order without chaos.

The idea of relation is also the first principle of social life, but here it is quickly transformed into organization. Organization is present as an aspect of the relations among individuals at every level of social life, from the mating pair and subsequent family to the nation-state and multinational corporation.

It should be pointed out that organization includes both the traditional arrangements and customs that have developed in response to various threats to survival (e.g., extended families, ritualized beliefs in messiahs or witches, food taboos), and the intentionally created superstructures of a society already self-consciously systematical (e.g., I.B.M., I.R.S., A.F.L.-C.I.O., the interstate highway system). In a nation of more than 200 million social beings, chaos is certain to break out frequently and irregularly—but order will recuperate and organization will recur because power abhors a vacuum. The dynamic of human organization is not the battle of power and morality, it is the battle of power and chaos.

Organization is an expression of our awareness that we are interdependent, and that in modern circumstances the very numbers of people make this interdependence essential for the maintenance of life. The recognition of this interdependent condition leads us to create the organizations necessary for accomplishing what the individual cannot do either alone or working independently in large numbers. This ability to organize for work in concert is the genius both of human civilization and of non-human civilization, such as the social systems of the ant, the bee, and the wolf.

The two oldest of human traits are the bases of our tendency to organize in response to the threat of chaos. One of these traits is the emotional disposition *to be related* with others in a bond of affinity; the other is the need *to be able* in accomplishing plans. The first is called love, the second power. In this view love and power are connected, not as opposites, but as the basic human elements in organized social life. Great acts of love, as well as acts of other kinds, depend for their realization on power.

The claim that love and power belong together may sound strange given the bias our culture has developed, following a biblical tradition, in separating the two as opposites. It would be more in keeping with this tradition to say that organized human life is based on love and threatened by power. There are other views of love—the Platonic, the Romantic, and the Freudian—that see it as a kind of power, or a context for power relations; but our culture has made it difficult to think of power in terms of love, or love in terms of power. It is usually assumed that power is the ethical antithesis of love, that it means hubris, a wanton disregard for others, violence, and selfish exploitation—immoral means to immoral gains. Power is often associated automatically with authoritarianism, and those who seem to covet (or simply to understand) power are met with furrowed brows and the straight-faced admonition that "love conquers all." The irony of such a ferocious notion of love, alas, goes unappreciated by the most earnest lovers of love.[10]

Organization and power are therefore conjugal concepts. They are bundled together. Where there is organization, there is power; where there is power, there is organization. If organization is inevitable in social life then it is also true that power is inevitable in all social relations. Power is present or potential as a quality of relationships not only in the courtrooms, war rooms, and boardrooms, but also in the nursery, kitchen, bedroom, schoolroom, and the ubiquitous waiting room, too.

Every organization is a matter of at least two people (but there is no maximum number) and at least one idea for action. Usually an organization operates with a system of ideas for a number of interrelated actions. These two factors make organization conceptually very similar to power, and the similarity holds as the elements of organization are expressed in more detail. At times, it is not clear whether there is a significant difference between saying something is "an organizational aspect of power," or a "power aspect of organization." These are words to be used in talking about each other.

Hierarchy. The people in an organization are usually related in a formal or informal ordering. Hierarchy is a ranked ordering, a system of priorities or prescriptions for attending to assignments, and for making the assignments in the first place. It is a principle of order which is close to the essence of governing in all of its familiar political forms. Furthermore, as Robert Michels[11] has pointed out, in all organizations of half a dozen or more members there seems to be an irresistible tendency toward an emergent leadership, toward oligarchy. On the face of it, this tendency (toward rule by the few) would seem to contradict democracy (rule by the many) but this conflict need not be serious when other aspects of power, namely, delegation and consent, are considered.

Mixed in with this "iron law of oligarchy" is another tendency, the inclination to distrust those in leadership positions when their lead is difficult to follow, or to swallow. In democratic, or demidemocratic arrangements, such distrust is organized in different ways—opposition parties, special interest groups, the journalistic media, dissenting intellectuals, and so on. This tendency to distrust individuals in a hierarchical system acts to guard the long-term interests of those who support a governing hierarchy. The hierarchy itself has become a permanent value in social life, inherent to organization just as organization is inherent to social relations, but any given set of individuals has only temporary tenure in the hierarchy. This is a formal representation of the great democratic principle of rule by law and not by individuals.

A central but seldom appreciated virtue of hierarchical organization is that individuals are vulnerable in direct relation to their visible responsibility. If someone can be identifed as responsible for X, and if X fails or is judged to be wrong, then the responsible individual can be held to account. This aspect of hierarchy may be more clearly appreciated when contrasted with another form of government control known as bureaucracy, or the "rule of an intricate system of bureaus in which no men, neither one nor the best, neither the few nor the many, can be held responsible, and which could properly be called rule by Nobody."[12] Hannah Arendt has suggested that this may be the most tyrannical of all forms of government:

If, in accord with traditional political thought, we identify tyranny as government that is not held to give account of itself, rule by Nobody is clearly the most tyrannical of all, since there is no one left who could even be asked to answer for what is being done. It is this state of affairs, making it impossible to localize responsibility and to identify the enemy, that is among the most potent causes of the current world-wide rebellious unrest, its chaotic nature, and its dangerous tendency to get out of control and to run amuck.[13]

Notice again the implied alternative of clear relations in visible, accountable, hierarchical organization as the answer to chaos. When the organization is dissipated and its identity dissembling, chaos creeps in like the London fog (of old) and obscures the rise of tyranny. Arendt's view runs close to the lines of Plato's argument that the excessive freedom of democracy leads inflexibly to despotism.[14]

Delegation and Consent. Hierarchy is a tendency to organize for leadership in concerted action. To act in concert requires some number of individuals and separate parts for them to play, and it requires agreement as to plan. In other words, it requires both delegation and consent.

The idea of delegation, or division of labor, is the heart of hierarchy and it is close to the heart of power, too. The person who has a plan and someone else who can help carry it out is more powerful than the person who has only a plan. The effectiveness of delegation depends on a group's acceptance of its leader and consent to the plan, at least as it affects individual obligations. Delegation works both from a group to the leader, as in electing a president who is thus delegated power to lead the electors, and from the leader to a group, as in a boss's giving orders to employees who must then perform their delegated labors. Both senses are governed by the same principles of division of labor and consent.

Every effective governing order, including the tyrannous, is dependent on acceptance, or the consent of the governed. The power of a governing order is great, but that power is grounded in majority consent that may at any time be withdrawn. In this way one can argue that the withdrawal of consent is the final power act. Consent is a form of control over power.

Authority is often said to be "legitimate" power. When a group acquiesces to power claims on grounds that these are acceptable and deserved, the group transforms power into authority. Authority based on forced acquiescence is tenuous for it is extremely vulnerable to the withdrawal of consent which can destroy it. Refusal to respect authority is the power over power which is present in the minds of all persons. Individual refusal to respect authority is not the same sort of power as organized refusal, but the two share a principle: power itself is delegated through consent, and without consent power inevitably is reduced to force, and thus eventually it is lost.

The Psychological Aspect of Power: Conformation of Consent

If delegation is central to understanding the social aspect of power, consent is central to understanding its psychological basis. Consent is the other side of delegation. Indeed, consent can be conceived as a sort of delegation—the delegation of power to the power claimant by way of accepting his claim. An elected official is delegated power by the voters who express their consent in votes; the official loses power when recalled or by failing to be re-elected. A boss exercises powers of delegation through the consent of the workers to work; the boss loses power through voluntary absenteeism, work slow-downs, sabotage, and strikes. The withdrawal of consent is the power most feared by the powerful.

Kinds of Consent. The complex concept of consent has two main categories of meaning: consenting attitudes and consenting actions. These categories can be separated for purposes of analysis of the concept, and it is possible to maintain that a consenting attitude need not lead to a consenting action, and that a consenting action can be effected without an attitude of consent. There are difficulties, however, in maintaining this distinction when one turns to the analysis of social events.

In political theory it is customary to think that the right to exercise authority is grounded in the attitude of consent. Political agency is a function of permission and the accord of various beliefs, just as authority is finally a function of respect. But beliefs may be held, permission and respect given, either passively or actively. Consent is an idea that takes many forms along a passive/active continuum, no single form of which can stand as the sole definition of consent, all forms of which are common to all social and political organizations.

The Consent Continuum. The forms of consent can be arranged on a scale defined by increasing degrees of willingness and the quality of information one has when deciding whether to give one's consent.

1. Acquiescence under threat of sanction. The form of least willing consent is forced obedience under threat of extreme sanction. One may have a choice only between consent and death or severe physical pain. A threat of force raises fear of certain violent consequences and this fear then produces desperate consent. Threats of moderate sanction work in a similar way. A person will consent to do (or not to do) something because the known consequence of not consenting is less desirable. A pupil will avoid detention by coming to class on time but reluctantly. It is force exhibited through the threat of sanction, whether extreme or moderate, that distinguishes this form of consent from the others. The threat of sanction also produces opposition and because of this, consent is won at the price of instability. Consent unwillingly given is but delayed opposition and must be maintained under constant watch and continued threat.

2. Compliance based on partial or slanted information. A person who is told that he now has "all the information he needs" to make a choice, and who doesn't realize that the in-

formation he does have is incomplete, or has been selected with bias, or carefully edited to serve the interest of those who control his access to that information, is likely to comply on what he takes to be rational grounds. This sort of compliance is the heart of all indoctrination and shows the enormous importance of the control of information in power relationships. Until recently parents of schoolchildren whose first language was not English accepted the placement of their children in remedial curriculum tracks based on IQ and achievement tests given in English. The State of California has challenged the legality and the morality of this procedure after establishing that the distribution of these same children when tested in their own first language was virtually the same as the distribution of children in other language groups.

3. Indifference due to habit and apathy. A person might follow the lead of someone just because there is no reason not to follow, or because one is used to being a follower. Such a person, if interested in anything, is probably most interested in avoiding the personal, social, and political entanglements that are inevitable when one participates in questions of who shall lead and for what reasons. I remember being "elected" to membership in an eating club at college because the club's president understood that his power was largely supported by the principle of apathy. When he wanted the membership to approve a proposal, as he did in the case of my candidacy, he would put the question this way: "Anyone *not* in favor please stand." Of course no one cared that much one way or the other, so the proposal passed.

4. Conformity to custom. A person may well believe that "what is done" is what others do, or have done. A disposition toward traditional obeisance is common not only among the religious but also among all those for whom it is important to be associated with stable groups of some kind. Having been raised in a certain tradition is sometimes enough to ensure continuous consent to that tradition and the demands of its arbiters. The same is true even for the casual conformists to

short-term contemporary norms and mores, those who have been thoroughly socialized *in* groups, but not always *as* groups. No one can avoid conformity altogether, one can only exercise some control over the object of one's conformity. Conformity to custom is perhaps the most common of all the forms of consent, and although it often is based on a rational understanding, this is not always the case. The lengthy continuous history of the Catholic Church is due largely to the membership's willingness to conform to certain of the church's expectations, for example, the promise to raise one's children in the Catholic faith regardless of whom one marries. While consent of this type is often rational and deferential, the extreme and bizarre "spiritual" cults of modern origin demand conformity so total as to be not only irrational but pathological. And of course the fashions of any given day command slaves enough to build pyramids.

5. Commitment through informed judgment. This type of consent is the ideal to which political theorists from Locke's time on have appealed in their defense of the democratic structuring of governmental authority; such consent represents an ideal more profoundly attractive than any other as the basis for a theory of government. Under this principle of consent through understanding, the informed majority delegates power deliberately, allowing for its temporary concentration in the hands of a few. When this contractual arrangement proves unsatisfactory to the majority of informed delegators, they collectively withdraw their consent from their chosen representatives and invest it in others. In a system based on this type of consent, protest can terminate authority peacefully because the protest is articulated through the procedures of legalized election.

Commitment through informed judgment is also an educational ideal, and it is in considering this type of consent that we see the link between education and the concepts of power and freedom. The nucleus of all three is information and its control. Indeed, one might read this consent continuum as a progression in the control of information and the formation of judgment. The last stage in the continuum describes the autonomous—that is, self-governing—individual who is capable of participating in rational deliberation, willing to make judgments based on that deliberation, and disposed to honor those judgments as personal commitments.

Of course this kind of informed judgment requires certain skills in reasoning and in using information to make plans and to resolve questions. These skills are at the core of any school curriculum designed for educational purposes in addition to socialization. In fact, one might say that the capacity to make autonomous and well-informed judgments, and the disposition to commit oneself to such judgments are central aims of education. The lesser forms of consent are more closely related to the aims of socialization, starting with the primitive use of threatened sanction, and leading up to the more civilized, but sometimes insidious, use of reward for conformity. Power is greatest when it employs the instruments of education, not the instruments of force or conformity. The instruments of education are designed to help individuals move from simple acquiescence all the way to the informed and critical approval of delegated authority—an approval based on the understanding that organized consent (and its withdrawal) is the ultimate source of all social power.

The Field of Consent.   A person may be asked for consent to any of three parts in a power relationship: the plan or system of ideas which is to be implemented, the person(s) in delegating positions, and the particular assignment given. Of these three the first is most interesting as a power variable.

There is a signal difference between the cooperation that can come from a shared understanding of ideas and values that are deemed to be personally important and philosophically significant and the compliance that comes from treating people merely as "behaving organisms." Since all human beings long for a sense of purpose as part of their lives and their labors, most people want to understand what they are doing, or why they are being asked to do it. Purposelessness, anomie, and alienation are symptoms of a modern illness caused by a deficiency of organizing ideas; the cure is meaning, that is, a hierarchy of values.

If people are treated merely as behaving organisms, as operational units, with no regard for their sense of purpose and their need to know, all that can be expected is temporary compliance and a tendency toward minimizing every effort— except the effort to escape from the power relationship. If people understand, or at least think they understand what is going on, why it is going on, and what part they play in a system of purposeful activity, the chances that cooperation will replace compliance increase considerably. In a limited but important way this need for a sense of purpose, which transforms mere compliance into cooperation and acts to keep the power-holders consistent in their actions, is the moral basis of power. Anyone interested in maintaining an institutional form of power would do well to keep in mind that consent informed by at least some understanding of the institution's purposes is necessary for both efficiency and stability.

While consent may be strong in this part of the power relationship, there may still be objections to the individuals who occupy positions of delegation (be they electors or bosses). Often the individual in charge of a cult, when it is new, is inseparable from its binding ideas and purpose, so to accept the purpose is to accept the leader, too. Christ was such a leader for his disciples, and so was Jim Jones for the members of the People's Temple. But in most institutions ideas and individuals are separate, and when there is conflict the individuals will change before the system of ideas does. A president is free to replace cabinet officers who disagree with his policy, for example. It is important to notice that even as individuals come and go, their institutional positions or roles remain, and are filled by other individuals.

Even when there is consent to the purposes of the institution and to the individuals who do the delegating, it is still possible to withhold consent from one's own particular assignment. This problem is not likely to be as serious as problems in the other two parts of the power relationship because one often feels a duty to do unchosen labor for people and purposes one can respect. The promise of a change in assignment for a job well done can of course be used as an incentive, but this tactic usually works only with the persons who already consent in general to the organization's purposes and its leaders.

Tactics of Withdrawal. One effective tactic for withdrawing consent is minimally organized dissent, not flagrant enough to attract punishment or personal acrimony, but sufficient to warn authorities that a protest is being made and claims to power challenged. Sneers, satire, and silence are all forms of such dissent, as is the "work slowdown," a situation in which the workers agree among themselves to do no more than the minimum as required by formal regulation. This tactic shows dramatically the importance of good will (and the potency of ill will) as the psychological basis of power.[15]

Saul Alinsky was a master of psychological power tactics, which he designed for use in organized community action groups. I recall hearing Alinsky explain a tactic that he never actually had to implement: it was so brilliantly conceived that the mere thought of it was enough to convince the late mayor of Chicago, Richard Daley, that he should comply with Alinsky's request to meet with the poor blacks whom Alinsky represented. The plan was simple. Alinsky studied the mayor to ascertain what was for him the proudest symbol of his administration's achievements, and found that it was O'Hare Airport, busiest in the world. The scheme was to make the nation laugh at O'Hare, and by extension, at Mayor Daley. Insult was the game, for as Alinsky knew well, power is secretly terrified of insult and ridicule.

Alinsky proposed to count all the toilets and urinals in the airport, and then to enlist enough constituents to provide one person for each toilet and two or three men for each urinal. On a given weekend, when passenger traffic was heavy with families and especially children, Alinsky's people would occupy all the toilet stalls and the men would stand in front of the urinals all day if necessary. In American society, one does not ask a gentleman to hurry up in such circumstances. There is really nothing one can say or do, except leave, avoiding the risk of embarrassing confrontation. No law is violated. The event is peaceful; except for the hundreds of seeping children and their vexed parents, and the thousands of travelers who most desperately need what O'Hare, for the first time, cannot provide.

The story (and pictures) of such a preposterous affair would have delighted viewers of the evening news in every state, and the sport made of Chicago would have driven Daley mad. Alinsky's telephone description of this perfectly legal insult and his promise that he already had two hundred or so volunteers was sufficient to break the Mayor's grip on power in this particular case and accomplish Alinsky's purpose. By himself Alinsky would have succeeded at no more than becoming a nuisance, but with a large organized social interest behind him he clearly demonstrated the power of withdrawing consent, even in quite ordinary circumstances.

Perhaps the ultimate in the withdrawal of consent is not revolution, recall, or insult, but laughter. Authority fears no threat more than the laughter that comes from scorn, for that which is scorned is not respected and authority cannot survive without respect. The regent whom the people ridicule in public will not be regent long; scorn is the scourge of power.

Obedience. On the face of it obedience seems a concept distant from consent. I would suggest, however, that obedience is a form of consent and that it deserves separate discussion for several reasons, the most important of which is its significance for education.

Étienne de la Boétie, a contemporary and friend of Montaigne, was the first to develop the insight that tyranny is always grounded in the general acceptance of tyranny. He was curious to know

> how it happens that so many men, so many villages, so many cities, so many nations, sometimes suffer under a single tyrant who has no other power than the power they give him; who is able to harm them only to the extent to which they have the willingness to bear with him; who could do them absolutely no injury unless they preferred to put up with him rather than contradict him. Surely a striking situation![16]

Assuming that no one would knowingly and willingly choose to relinquish power to a tyrant, la Boétie suggested that force and deception are the two major factors that lead to such mass obedience. He touched the heart of the problem when he added that those who lose their liberty through deceit are "not so often betrayed by others as misled by themselves."[17] Like Mithridates, who trained himself to drink poison, those who give away their power do so through an unthinking, gradual habituation to servitude. La Boétie viewed self-deception as the greatest enemy of freedom. Passive consent to the way things are soon becomes absolute obedience; it is the tyrant's best friend, whereas education about the nature of consent, freedom, and power is his greatest enemy.

Faced with the enigma of mass civil obedience, la Boétie wrote the first protocol for mass civil *dis*obedience, a call that was relayed to Gandhi through Tolstoy. He emphasized the instrumental importance of education for the subjects of tyranny—they had to be taught to understand that mass civil disobedience, the organized withdrawal of their consent, is the only remedy for state tyranny, and that they had thoughtlessly deceived themselves into the condition of obedience which makes tyranny possible. Control of education, la Boétie insisted, is closely related to the control of power and freedom.

Civil obedience is support for the tyrant, just as it is the foundation of support for any state. Obedience per se is neither a wholly bad nor wholly good relationship. It is important to say, as la Boétie failed to, that there are occasions that require obedience if freedom is to be exercised and tyranny controlled. That we obey traffic laws and rely on others to do the same is the essence of one's "freedom of the road"; everyone is equally constrained by a public system of rules, rather than acting according to an individual code. Exceptions are always hazardous in traffic and sometimes in government—for example, when "executive privilege" is abused for purposes of self-aggrandizement.

However, the larger point is clear: we cannot excuse the paradigmatic criminal obedience of an Adolf Eichmann on the grounds he offered, namely: (1) it was his duty to obey orders and the laws (acts of state); (2) he was no one to judge, or even have his own thoughts on the matter of the orders he was asked to execute; (3) obedience to superiors had always been praised as a virtue and he was trying to be virtuous; and (4) he was not acting as an individual man but as a functionary whose actions could easily have been carried out by (many) others.

In political circumstances obedience is support, no matter how great the psychological distance one achieves from one's actions. Eichmann's dissociation from the meaning of his action was not his evil genius nor was it his evil ignorance—he was a man of ordinary intelligence. His dissociation was his thoughtlessness and his inability to withdraw consent, to disobey what he had previously agreed to without full understanding. Hannah Arendt has made an observation on obedience that is worth preserving: the thoughtlessness of the obedient one is what makes obedience to evil tyrants so dangerous, and this same ordinary thoughtlessness makes evil of Eichmann's kind banal.[18] Such unwillingness or inability to think about what one is doing, to comprehend the morality of one's actions, and to understand how a power relationship educes obedience is an educational problem of greater seriousness than any other. Thoughtless obedience is potentially the most lethal form of consent, and its only known cure is learning to think—about power and powerlessness.

Stanley Milgram's empirical studies[19] of Arendt's observations have shown that an appalling number of "average" Americans easily give away control of their own behavior and become utensils for carrying out the wishes, the "orders," of presumed "authorities" whom they have agreed to obey without coercion of any sort. (In fact, Milgram's subjects were paid $4 and carfare for volunteering to participate in "a psychological experiment in memory and learning.") Milgram's data, gathered from more than a thousand people—men and women, young and old, blue- and white-collar, poor and wealthy—chill the imagination and wreck the theory that Eichmann was a uniquely perverted villian who had nothing in common with the mailman, our teachers, friends, and neighbors.

The basic experiment was simple:

> Two people come to a psychological laboratory to take part in a study of memory and learning. One of them is designated as a "teacher" and the other a "learner." The experimenter explains that the study is concerned with the effects of punishment on learning. The learner is conducted into a room, seated in a chair, his arms strapped to prevent excessive movement, and an electrode attached to his wrist. He is told that he is to learn a list of word pairs; whenever he makes an error, he will receive electric shocks of increasing intensity.[20]

The "teacher" sees all this, but he does not know that the "learner," a middle-aged man, is an actor in cahoots with the experimenter and that he actually receives no shock at all. The "teacher" is seated at his station in another room where he is confronted with a shock generator that has switches designated in 15-volt increments from 15 to 450 volts. The high end switches are marked "Danger!" in red. The "teacher" is to administer a shock for every wrong answer he gets from the "learner," each time increasing the voltage by one increment.

Milgram states that conflict arises

> when the man receiving the shock begins to indicate that he is
> experiencing discomfort. At 75 volts, the "learner" grunts. At 120
> volts he complains verbally; at 150 he demands to be released
> from the experiment. His protests continue as the shocks escalate,
> growing increasingly vehement and emotional. At 285 volts his
> response can only be described as an agonized scream.[21]

Eventually (after 330 volts) he falls silent and his answers no
longer appear on the signal box.

If the "teacher" indicated at any time that he (or she) did not
wish to go on, the experimenter said:

1) Please continue, or Please go on.
2) The experiment requires that you continue.
3) It is absolutely essential that you continue.
4) You have no other choice, you *must* go on.[22]

The chief finding of this study is the extreme willingness of
American adults to follow commands, mild as they were and
carrying no punitive sanction, issued by someone whom they
perceived as an authority. Nearly "two-thirds of the participants fall into the category of 'obedient' subjects, and . . . they
represented ordinary people drawn from working, managerial,
and professional classes."[23] This is not to say that the participants did not suffer great tension because they were violating
their own fundamental moral standards, for many did. It is to
say, however, that even when this was the case only a few
people had the resources to challenge the power they had delegated to the experimenter. Two-thirds of the participants were
made powerless on the spot, having donated their sense of responsibility to the authority when asked to do so. The experi-
ments never threatened them, yet they obeyed, some with sorrow, because they did not understand the dynamic principles of
a power relationship.

Obedience is delegating to another the power of control over one's behavior; it is divesting oneself of the responsibility and the initiative to make judgments. La Boétie, Arendt, and Milgram help make the case that thoughtless obedience is an urgent educational problem and that study of the power/powerlessness relation is a salient educational concern. Educators who persist in ignoring the study of power are a tyrant's delight and a peril to democracy.

The Instrumental Aspect of Power

Power is pragmatic. It is a term that cannot be understood apart from practical bearings. Power is always found in relation, not in isolation, and its presence is measured by reference to effect and consequences. Although power is sometimes spoken of as an end in itself, or as a personality trait, or motive, or even as some sort of metaphysical entity, it is better represented and better understood when spoken of as a means.

Power is used primarily as a noun in English, a fact that inhibits our ability to think clearly about the concept. While a transitive verb form is listed as obsolete in *Webster's New International Dictionary,* Second Edition, the Third Edition drops that designation and lists additional meanings—"to give strength to," "to supply with or propel by means of motive power," "to give impetus to." But the fact remains that in discussing power as an aspect of social relations, its noun form predominates. One rarely, if ever, hears the transitive verb form in use. Cousin terms like "influence," "control," and "force" have common noun and verb forms, but power does not. It should. If we think of power as a noun, as a thing, it is difficult to bear in mind that power is a quality of relations—it is a relational concept that is part of any context that includes at least two people and one intended action. Power is an aspect of the transaction-in-context, it is part of the action. It designates the expression of means or agency.

Power language is the language of problem-solving. It is useful to the degree that it helps to show just how a problem and a subsequent plan of action are set up and how the individuals involved are related to it and to each other. The instrumental aspect of power is perhaps most easily understood in relation to the philosophy of pragmatism: a focus on intelligently controlled purposive action in a social context, and on planned effort to produce intended consequences in that context. Pragmatism is a philosophy of agency and practical effect; it is an action philosophy at home in the busy and constant transactions among mind, self, and society. Pragmatism emphasizes the thinking person's ability to imagine circumstances that do not yet exist, to plan the realization of what has been imagined, and through cooperation to achieve that planned set of circumstances. In short, pragmatism is interested in the exercise of ability in a context of social relations. It is the philosophy of ordering chaos incrementally, the philosophy of power.

As a way to see the value of a verb form for power, it is useful to borrow the language of pragmatism on the subject of means and ends (verbs and nouns). This language reflects the point of view that ends and means are in a relation of continual transformation, and that the distinction between them is both temporal and relational. Once an end-in-view is achieved, it joins the antecedent conditions for the next end-in-view, and therefore constitutes part of the means to that end. Similarly, means transform the ends they produce by the very nature of their influence (a means is a change). Since power is instrumental in achieving intended consequences (ends), it is in turn contained in those consequences. Power is therefore inherent in all social transaction, and, whenever it is present as actuality or potential, we measure it in terms of the further consequences it produces.

There is, however, a distinction to be made between power's short-term and long-term consequences—a distinction that limits the power any particular agent can hold. Simply put, short-term events can be pretty well controlled, but long-term events (or long-range consequences) cannot. As Berle has pointed out:

> One impact of power holding on the holder is his discovery that the power act, the direction of an event, causes surprisingly unpredictable consequences. . . . The power to cause an event has scant relation to capacity to control the feelings and opinions of men about the thing done, or assure their adhesion to a larger plan.[24]

Predictability is the guardian of power, but in the long run it cannot protect power against its own fickle effects. This situation should be a comfort to those who fear that we face a future of stable, concentrated power monopolies.

In attempting to understand power it is important to remember that as an instrumental aspect of social relations power is contingent on the always mutable details of those relations. As a result power should be thought of as temporal and relational; its fluctuations parallel those between ends and means. Power always occurs in relation to powerlessness, but the relative dimensions of power and powerlessness are continually being rearranged, readjusted. If only two people were related through only one plan, then the power/powerlessness balance would be clear and highly predictable. But social life is much more complex than that. Every person is related to many others through many plans, and any individual will be powerful or powerless depending on the circumstances and the particular people and plans in question. In the course of a single day one can act as a grandson, son, brother, husband, father, boss, employee, taxpayer, coach, shortstop, customer, passenger, driver, and patron with vastly different instrumental effects and manifestations of power. Powerlessness means not being able and it suggests a sense of personal insignificance in all sorts of planned action. When one cannot affect the instrumental aspects of social relations, and when this inability is felt as a loss of significance, the result is powerlessness.

Summary: The Configuration of Power

This analysis of power has not produced a strict definitional closure, but it has developed a set of specifications and a pattern of meaning which challenge the putative understanding of power. My purpose has been to sharpen our analytical ability to perceive the several aspects of power in social relations, not to reduce the idea to another brittle, splintered stipulation. Fundamentally important social ideas like power are inclusive—they are so central to life that all of life's variety must be contained in their definitions if the definitions are to be wholly accurate and satisfying. It would seem that aiming for a total definition of power is rather like aiming for the stars—all of them at once—with arrows.

I have tried to show that Acton's apothegm, while entertaining, is not especially useful as a general proposition about power. Among the proposals offered in establishing my point of view were these:

1. Power is only one of many sources of human corruption, and in fact powerlessness may be more often and more violently corrupting than power.

2. The idea of relation (organization) is the first principle of social life, and two equally primitive and genuine categories of human experience lie beneath organization (as an answer to chaos). These are love (the disposition to be related with others in a bond of closeness in feeling), and power (the motive and capacity to accomplish plans with others). These two traits are not necessarily antithetical and can be complementary.

3. Order, organization, and therefore power are universally inherent in social life, because wherever there is organization there is power, and vice versa. Organization and power are conjugal concepts.

4. The minimum necessary conditions for actual or potential power are two people and one plan for action. These conditions mean that power is always partly social, partly psychological, and invariably instrumental. The social aspect is marked by

hierarchy, delegation, and cooperation; the psychological aspect is identified with several forms of consent (including obedience) and the withdrawal of consent. The instrumental aspect is a blend of the pragmatic principles that govern rational problem-solving—the exercise of executive abilities in a social context by way of cooperative effort in accomplishing plans of action.

5. Power has no commonly used verb form in English, even though it is preeminently an action concept, and this inhibits the understanding of power.

6. Any power-holder is limited by the unpredictability of power's long-term effects, and by the consent (good will) of those who delegate the power.

7. A great deal of power's meaning lies in its instrumental significance. The anti-power concept that makes most sense, given this analysis, is not "morality" (as certain self-consciously moralistic traditions would have it) but instrumental insignificance.

Although this analysis has produced only a configuration of power and not a new definition, it would be an error to conclude that, because power cannot be securely gripped in language, we would spend our time more wisely if we stopped trying to understand it. Whether well understood or not, power plays a serious part in all aspects of our lives, but if we keep our attention fresh and our debate lively we may reach a fuller understanding—an understanding that can help someone to imagine the means for transforming the conditions that cause so much unnecessary pain, odium, and shame. We cannot avoid being affected by power, we can only avoid thinking about it. The greater danger is not the growth of power, but foolishness. As G. B. Shaw reminds us: "Power does not corrupt men; fools, however, if they get into a position of power, corrupt power."[25]

3 /

Power and Education

Why is power not included in the lexicon of educators? The idea of power has been more completely neglected in education studies than in any other discipline of fundamental social interest. Power talk is conspicuously absent from schools and from educational literature; indeed, one is more likely to hear singing in a bank than serious talk of power in relation to education.

This claim may seem off the mark to readers who have seen such books as Brameld's *Education as Power,* Czartoryski's *Education for Power,* or Baldridge's *Power and Conflict in the University.* Surely these titles would indicate that power *has* been studied and analyzed as a concept in education. This is the view taken by some colleagues in educational studies who direct our attention to the dozens of books on education dealing with control, planned change, autonomy, authority, governance, management, and so on. Of course this argument is true, but it is beside the point if these books deal with their topics without analyzing power per se. Books such as *Power, Presidents, and Professors,* and *Power and Conflict in the University* are cited as examples, but titles can be misleading, especially if they include the word "power." Here is a brief annotated list of books that should help to make clear the difficulty.

Power, Presidents, and Professors, by N. J. Demerath, R. W. Stephens, and R. R. Taylor (Basic Books, 1967), includes a brief summary (6 pages) of a survey done on the question of the degree to which "esteem" is correlated with "decision-making influence" as an index of power in academic departments. But nowhere is there an analysis of what power means, or how it is related conceptually to esteem, decision-making influence, or anything else. The book is not about power at all; it is about university administrative organization.

Power and Conflict in the University, by J. V. Baldridge (Wiley, 1971), makes an allusion to the Hunter, Dahl, and Polsby studies in "community power," and describes some work done in social psychology on "power in groups" (Cartwright, French, and Raven). Elsewhere, "power" turns up unsystematically in such phrases as "student power," "power plays," "powerful people," and so on. Baldridge's interest is not in the analysis of power, but in academic governance and decision-making in universities.

Power and Authority: Transformation of Campus Governance, edited by H. L. Hodgkinson and L. R. Meeth (Jossey-Bass, 1971), contains twelve essays, of which five have "power" in their titles, but only one definition of power, and no discussion of the concept at all.

Power and Process: The Formulation and Limits of Federal Educational Policy, by H. L. Summerfield (McCutchan, 1974), is not about the concept of power, but rather about the role and process of government policymaking.

Education as Power, by T. Brameld (Holt, Rinehart and Winston, 1965), offers no definition and no analysis of power other than a seven-page statement agreeing with Bacon's dictum that "knowledge is power." Brameld argues that both power—whatever that means—and knowledge should be used for the moral purposes of a "democratic world order."

Education for Power, by A. Czartoryski (Davis-Poynter, 1975), posits power as "the name we give to the relationship between the dominating and the dominated," and goes on to argue for an active, participatory democracy. The author rightly notes that power is inherent in social organization, but narrowly construes power to be always corrupting and self-serving—"power extirpates from the mind every humane and gentle virtue."[1] This observation is the extent of his investigation of power.

Power to Change: Issues for the Innovative Educator, edited by C. M. Culver and G. J. Hoban (McGraw-Hill, 1973), offers no definition and no analysis of power.

Power to the Teacher: How America's Educators Became Militant, by M. O. Donley, Jr. (Indiana University Press/Phi Delta Kappa, 1976), does not even list power in the index. The book is a description of the growth of the NEA, AFT, and other teacher unions.

The list could be longer, but there is no need to continue. The point is that the appearance of "power" in the title of a book is no proof that the concept has been treated seriously within. I might conclude this cursory survey with a word about the collection of essays called *Power and Ideology in Education,* edited by J. Karabel and A. H. Halsey. Power is an explicit, if unanalyzed theme in the contributions by Basil Bernstein and that of Pierre Bourdieu. Their research on the relations between the contents of knowledge and the "structure of power" in society is perhaps the most promising attempt to increase our understanding of the concept of power in education. Bernstein in particular seems on track in his studies of the principles of power which lie embedded in the language of education and the organization of controlled information in the school curriculum. But as Bernstein himself has pointed out, one of the main unresolved problems of his work is how "power relationships penetrate the organization, distribution and evaluation of knowledge through the social context."[2]

There are indeed many books and articles in educational studies that use the word "power"—still there are none that provide a sustained analysis of the concept itself. One has to look at the various social sciences and political philosophy for such analyses, and even then there are difficulties, as I showed earlier.

While it is true that one group of educators thinks that the meaning of power is obvious, well understood, and in some sense fixed into place by these "dozens of books" on change, governance, and management, there is another and I think larger group that reacts quite differently to the subject of power in educational theory.

I recall trying to discuss power and its usefulness as a concept for analyzing education with a retired professor and dean of students at one of this country's leading colleges. She was a scholar of undisputed influence, a teacher whose rigorous standards and success with students were well known, and a dean much admired (even feared by some) for her skills in resolving troublesome issues, yet she was horrified (discreetly, but horrified) at my suggestion that power is inherent in the character of education, and that, given her experience, she was in a favored position to know a lot about it.

Maintaining that I should know better, being a teacher myself, she argued that as educators we try to accomplish a planned set of changes in our students. She agreed that we do this by means of influence, motivation, and even sanction, but insisted that our work is an ethical contribution to individual and social well-being, not an expression of power. Yes, she agreed, the effects of "having" an education, especially a college education, are socially and financially significant for a considerable number of graduates, in particular those who are subsequently employed in large and influential organizations. But she believed that education worked only for the containment of power; the control of force by intelligence and character.

We spoke on many other themes, including her belief that a good teacher never has to use power—except, possibly, as a last resort in extraordinary circumstances. Before we parted she admonished to be careful when introducing power to other educators because they would be as reluctant as she to accept it as a concept appropriate to the analysis of their professional views and experiences. But she also conceded that her own conception of power had changed during our talk, and that the conception of power I had advanced could be appropriate for educational analysis.

This example illustrates that there is a radical conflict in the minds of educators between their notions of their own work and their concept of power. This enmity between education and power is like that between love and power—deep and mistaken. Although such a conflict makes it difficult to think about power in relation to education, it is important that we begin to do so.

The Expurgated Version of Educational Philosophy

The first attempt to analyze the idea of power which I know of is Plato's account of a dispute between Socrates and Polus, who is joined by Callicles, in the dialogue called *Gorgias*.[3] This early analysis marked the beginning of the enduring expurgation of power from the philosophy of education.

Polus, certainly not one of Socrates' more formidable debate partners, reflects a common view of power in his envy of it, and in his belief that happiness depends on having (a lot of) it. Having power, for Polus, means that he must do only what seems best to him; it means being at liberty to do as he pleases in the state. Socrates links this view of power with the orators and tyrants who commit great crimes with their "liberty" to follow their own pleasure.

Polus' line of thought is that being able to do as one pleases means having power, and having power means being happy, for doing as one pleases is what he understands happiness to be. Socrates, however, points out that an unintelligent (or uneducated) person may very well wish to do something that is not good—that will not bring him advantage. In fact what this person chooses to do may bring punishment and great unhappiness. If having power is merely being able to do as one pleases, then, for some it is likely to lead not to happiness, but to wretchedness.

Socrates would have Polus understand the difference between doing what one wants, regardless of what that may be, and doing what is good—that is, being willing to do what is wise and just. Drawing on this distinction, Socrates sets up an opposition between power (doing what one wants, and the possibility of eventual suffering), and education (coming to will what is wise and just, which is the good that brings happiness). This contrast in views is clearly illustrated when Polus asks Socrates whether he thinks the Great King (Archelaus of Macedonia) is happy. Socrates replies that he cannot say because he does not know about the king's education or how he stands on justice. These are the two criteria that, for Socrates, account for all true happiness.

The comparison made in this exchange suggests a division deeper than mere disagreement over a single concept; it represents two profoundly divergent attitudes about life, human nature, and the prospects for happiness. Later in the dialogue, Callicles takes up the argument begun by Polus and develops it into the view that the will to power can be derived from nature itself—from the very struggle for existence. This is an argument for the "natural" distribution of power to the strongest individuals in that struggle. It amounts to a justification for the use of force, as a form of power, in the activities of survival. It is an argument based on an identification of power with force, which is a mistake.

The significance of this mistake becomes clear as Callicles argues that any social theory constructed from his idea of power would relegate education to a minor role, because the philosophy of culture, or education, is the calculated undoing of the natural. Therefore, education can serve only to take power from the strong (who have made a successful "natural" claim to it) and give it to the weak. In his way of thinking, education would turn power on its head (as Socrates put Callicles on *his* head by the end of their debate).

Werner Jaeger's comments on this dispute summarize it concisely:

> In this comparison between two diametrically opposite philosophies of life, the two concepts of *paideia* and *power* are sharply

contrasted: and with good reason. Apparently they have little to do with each other. But (as the passage shows) Plato takes them to be opposing conceptions of human happiness—which means, of human nature. We have to choose between the philosophy of power and the philosophy of culture. . . . The philosophy of power is the doctrine of force. It sees war and conquest everywhere in life, and believes that that sanctions the use of force. It can have no meaning except through the seizure of the greatest possible power. The philosophy of culture or education asserts that man has a different aim: *kalokagathia*. Plato defines it as the opposite of injustice and wickedness—it is therefore essentially a matter of ethics.[4]

Do we have to choose between the philosophy of power and the philosophy of culture or education? If we are like Socrates and Callicles in their misunderstanding of power, we do have to face this choice, and the result will likely be the same: the expurgation of power from philosophy of education on grounds that they are ethically incompatible. But power and philosophy of education are opposed only if we accept this view that power is the doctrine of force and education is a (separate) matter of ethics. I have no trouble thinking of education and the philosophy of education as inherently ethical because any act undertaken with the purpose of influencing and changing a person, or group of persons, to be "better off" is inherently ethical. The particular moral character of an educational theory depends on its definition of "better off," and its recommended means. But if power is understood to be a complex, omnipresent aspect of social life itself, then it would seem that any serious reckoning of education could not avoid speaking to several distinctive issues of power.

In my judgment, philosophy of education has been dogged in its denial of power, both as a characteristic of relations within education, and as an aspect of relations between education and the rest of social life. This denial has a history that stretches from Plato to the present, and a psychology that is constrained by wishful thinking—wishing not to know those facts of social psychology that may abrade good intentions. Wishful thinking is a defense against looking for the truth, and as such it is incompatible with philosophy of all kinds and philosophy of education in particular.

It does no good simply to assert that one must choose between the philosophy of power and the philosophy of education; that power should have no place in education; and that the aims of one are antithetical to the aims of the other. Such wishful thinking beguiles educators into abdicating any responsibility for teaching how to channel existing power constructively. Tyrannous governments are of course delighted with this abdication and are most willing to reinforce it along with other forms of the compliant and self-defeating wish not to know. To think, then, that education is somehow alien and superior to all considerations of power is more than mere wishful thinking. It is an overweening and hazardous conceit that puts any design for democracy at risk. I take the position that thinking about education will be enriched by a redintegration of power in educational philosophy. "Redintegration" is a useful term that is seldom used. It carries the meaning of reconciliation and the strong implication of a return to a condition of soundness, wholeness, and integrity. It suits precisely my intention to suggest ways in which the idea of power may be applied to a renovation of educational philosophy.

I must now try to identify the basic forms of power, consider their differences, and establish the groundwork for their place in this renovation.

The Forms of Power

Force. The most primitive and least stable form of power is that occurring when actual or threatened physical harm is used to force consent (obedience) from the otherwise unwilling. Usually, it is the threat, rather than the actual use of force which induces obedient consent, and consent so won is contingent on the continued presence of the threat. This contingency makes the force form of power inherently unstable because threats produce hostility in those who are threatened, hostility that may at any time be turned against the power-wielder. Power gained by force is also costly and inefficient because unwilling, hostile consent must be maintained under constant surveillance—a situation that requires a large investment of resources. As Milton put it in *Paradise Lost:* "Who overcomes by force, hath overcome but half his foe."

Force appears at every level of social life. Indeed, there are so many familiar examples—from the neighborhood bully to the organized violence of military governments—that they hardly need enumeration or explanation. I would go further and say that there is a strong cultural tendency in America to equate power with force, perhaps because force is so blatant, so easy to recognize, and relatively easy to understand. My purpose in what follows is to expose and weaken this tendency by considering three more forms of power that are not so immediately obvious, but which I believe are even more important for us to understand.

Fiction. The central task in the exercise of power is eliciting from others the consent necessary to put one's plan into effect. One can force consent with threatened or actual physical harm, but it can be won with words and ideas and images, too. A person who is good at using words to turn ideas into images in the minds of listeners and readers—a storyteller—is a person of great potential power.

I should say that I understand "story" to include all of the meanings that are reported in *Webster's New International Dictionary,* Second Edition: (a) a connected narration of past events, (b) an account or recital of some incident or event, a report, (c) a narrative or tale, (d) a falsehood, (e) a tradition or legend, (f) a news article. In this broad sense "story" describes all kinds of verbal expression, from history and philosophy to fantasy and lies. (Some would not take that to be a very broad range, I know.)[5]

It is important to think of a storyteller as someone who uses words to create a sense of meaning, or a structure to use for interpreting a collection of events. All such senses or structures of meaning are inventions; they are created for the purpose of helping to sort out and evaluate different bits of experience. These inventions are, in an important way, the necessary fictions of mental life. We cannot live without them—or at least we cannot live and communicate together without them.

Stories, then, and storytellers purvey their power by creating ways of thinking about certain plans. They are agents of change, calling for conditional assent to a way of thinking. If the key to an effective power relationship is eliciting consent to help achieve a plan for action, one good way to get that consent is to create a belief in the plan itself. This can be done by telling stories that appeal somehow to the core of meanings that support and transform beliefs. A good storyteller can induce belief and arouse commitment in the listener.

We should not equate the fiction form of power with deliberate deception and ignoble propaganda, for it is much more versatile than that, capable of dealing with many subjects and many purposes. While it is clear that politicians use this form of power to win elections, raise taxes, and make war, it is less clear—but no less true—that scientists use it to introduce new theories and explanations of the nature of things, be they microphysical (do you believe in "quarks"?) or astrophysical ("quasars"? "black holes"?). Then we have the metaphysical philosophers whose stories about "quintessences" are still taken seriously by some.

Teachers use their own stories, too, as pedagogical techniques in motivating students to do better than the students believe they can. Every history book is composed of stories (conceptual structures invented to help interpret events—"The Dark Ages," "The Causes of the Civil War," "Republicanism," "The Cold War"). Indeed, the curriculum itself is a fictional structure invented for the purpose of interpreting a collection of experiences as "education." To accept a curriculum, to believe that it represents the meaning of education, is to consent to the curriculum designers' plan for action and to help perform it.

Every story has a plot. That is to say, every collection of related events has some sense of meaning that governs the structure of its relations. Events without plot make no more sense than reasons without argument, or education without purpose. Plotting is a mental activity; it exists in the minds of the storyteller and the listener, the partners in serious discussion, the educator and the student. Of course, sometimes it's not the *same* plot that each has in mind, but each acts according to *some* plot, otherwise events would produce no meaning at all. When the plots are very different, as would be the case in a successful con-job or an effective conspiracy, the crucial function of plotting becomes obvious. In both literary composition and educational philosophy, on the other hand, the importance of plotting is not always so clear to the naïve reader or to the uninitiated student. The plot of a story (or an educational scheme) exists in the author's (educational philosopher's) mind as he designs and interprets the narrative's (curriculum's) patterned arrangement. If the reader (student) comes to engage in a similar plotting activity and thereby gains an understanding of the structure that imparts meaning to the separate events, then to that extent the story (education) is successful, and the plot clear. Understanding the plot of a story or an education is thus an achievement that goes far beyond the mere perception of a sequence of events.

Statements of educational purpose can themselves be read as stories. The trick is to figure out the plot that governs the purposes as they are shaped into argument and policy. Purposes are set up as objects, or objectives, to be attained; they are specified and intended actions, or events. And like the actions or events in any other kind of story, they require some sort of plot to make sense. We have been asking "What is the story with American education?" for many years. We should now be asking "What is the educational plot in America?" Without knowing the plot how are we to make sense of the particular actions and events that make up these stories?

A foreign language requirement, a physical education program, desegregation plans, a seminar on Catullus, "family health" classes, IQ testing, special classes in ninth-grade English for college students (with credit toward graduation), reform in property tax based school finance, the PTA, a delinquent doodler diagraming sentences at the board after school—none of these educational events makes sense on its own. Even when these events are embedded in yet other events, and surrounded by plenty of plausible purposes, the meaning of the story that they compose is not yet clear, because the plot remains unknown. Are foreign language requirements, Catullus, and IQ testing connected more closely with each other than with any other events in the list? Do desegregation plans, special classes in ninth-grade English for college students, and tax reform fit together? What link is there between physical education, family health, and the PTA? Is it always more important to diagram than to doodle? Are all of these parts of a single epic? A cabala? A serial? None of these questions can be answered or even analyzed for educational significance unless and until a plot has been revealed, that is, until one knows which sense of meaning shaped the relations among the various educational events.

Appeals to educational stories (statements of purpose, descriptions of events) work well to induce belief and arouse commitment—in Congress and in classrooms. The stories and the effects they produce (e.g., deception, motivation, inspiration) are themselves aspects of power which influence and sometimes control power relations. To understand these relations, one must understand the plot that organizes the story's events. One must ask who is involved, what is the plan for action (the intent), and how the individuals are related to each other in light of the plan. These are questions about plot per se; they are also questions about the basis of all social relations of which power is an aspect. In this way plot and power are related in the analysis of educational stories.

Both noble and ignoble cousins lodge in power's fictional forms, in plots conveyed by stories that are told to induce particular cognitive and emotional effects. Lying belongs here, as do other forms of deception; but so do motivation and lofty inspiration. Whether one makes intentionally inaccurate statements about one's knowledge, or accurate ones; whether one speaks an imagined truth or a proven one; whether one aims at another's vulnerabilities or strengths—in all cases, if one is trying to enlist the cooperation of the other person for purposes of accomplishing a plan for action, then one is using fiction as a form of power. The politician who rallies the nation to support a war it does not want by telling lies about the "enemy aggressor," by telling stories of jingoistic heroes, the philosopher who placates millions by arguing that history has a mind of its own and that mere human individuals can do nothing to change the "inevitable flow" of "the forces" of determinism, the priest who reiterates the orthodoxies of his holy book and secures the faith of hundreds, the teacher who convinces students that they can do better work than they ever thought they could, boosting motivation with words, expecting more of them and acting as if they will succeed, and the conman who can sell something to almost every one of us if we listen long enough to his seductive tale—these are all examples of the power of fiction.

Finance. After force and fiction comes finance, the third general class of power relations. Finance is most easily understood and commonly recognized as an offer of reward for services made within the rules of some theory of economic exchange. The reward need not be money, but it must always be something valued by the one who performs the service, just as the service must be valued by the one who offers the reward. In short, cooperation is achieved by the exchange of costs and benefits.

I have chosen finance (the science of revenue, or income from any source) as the name for this form to avoid too close an association with economic and exchange theories of power (while borrowing some ideas from them).[6] In the simplest of words, this form of power involves offering or withholding rewards to people in order to make social conditions more consistent with a particular plan. In power relations of this sort, consent is bought. An employer buys time and labor from individuals with wages. A warden buys good behavior from prisoners with a reduction in sentence or parole. A military officer buys extra effort from his men with promotions and medals. An animal trainer buys obedience with bits of sugar and affection.

In education, the finance form of power can be seen in the assignment of grades, promotions, honors, recommendations, and the like in exchange for hard work, high achievement, and good behavior. All that, I think, is obvious enough not to require argument. Perhaps less obvious, but more interesting for power theory, is the practice of behavioral modification programs.

The manipulation of costs and benefits is the talent of market modification. The manipulation of contingencies and reinforcement is the talent of behavior modification. This particular psychological theory, which has found recent wide favor in the schools, is a variation of exchange theory. The power of both consists in restricting the range of choices open to others by using a variety of means for contingency management and selective reinforcement. Theoretically, perfect control of a given set of contingencies will yield perfectly predictable behavior, the behavioral science equivalent of a market monopoly (raising similar questions about anti-trust violation?). Empirically, however, and thank God, such perfect control of behavior is not possible in ordinary life because not all relevant contingencies can be managed perfectly at one time.

Teachers do control rewards in classrooms, however imperfectly, as a general feature of most that goes on there. And to the extent that the teacher is able to enlist the cooperation of students in adopting the teacher's plan for action, the teacher is exercising power.

Very young students learn that schools are serious places as soon as they begin to experience what it is like to live in conditions of constant observation and evaluation. Such assessment by others is crucial to these students, but the evaluations made by their teachers are the most crucial of all. Peers also evaluate, and self-evaluation develops, too, but things in school happen because the teacher makes them happen. The power behind this control is not lost on even the dullest of students. When they come to school, from the first day of kindergarten, students learn to do what the teacher and other adults at the school tell them to do. First they learn merely to do what they are told regardless of how they feel about it, but later on they learn to do what they are bid with enthusiasm, gladly and energetically. They learn, in other words, that certain kinds of consent are more highly rewarded than others. Cheerful compliance wins out over reluctant caving-in.

In learning these techniques students are at the same time learning to accept and adopt the teacher's plan for action even when it means surrendering their own. This process is an early lesson in the basics of power relations. Insofar as the teacher is able to enlist the cooperation of students in adopting his or her plan for action, the teacher is exercising power. Students may learn to cooperate because they recognize that good behavior pays off. A student becomes school-wise by learning the skills of compliance and cooperation with the teacher's plan.

One of the first and most obvious jobs a student has to accomplish in adjusting to school is learning

> to behave in such a way as to enhance the likelihood of praise and reduce the likelihood of punishment. In other words, he must learn how the reward system of the classroom operates and then use that knowledge to increase the flow of rewards to himself.[7]

Adaptation to the teacher's power of delegation is a major task of all students. In this way of thinking, the teacher is like a banker who controls evaluation, which is the currency of the classroom (and greater educational) economy. To push the analogy one small step further, one could say the evaluations are loan notes that the student repays with interest, and which may be called in by the bank at any time. In this system of exchange it is very likely that if the student shows great interest, i.e., pays a lot of attention, then the loan of a positive evaluation is secure.

The system of rewards in which students and teachers find themselves operates with regard to two curricula: the overt one of educational objectives, and the hidden one of classroom custom and institutional mores. It becomes apparent early in the school year who the "good" and "not-so-good" students are because the evaluations of educational performance are often public. In addition,

> every school child quickly learns what makes teachers angry. He learns that in most classrooms the behavior that triggers the teacher's ire has little to do with wrong answers or other indicators of scholastic failure. Rather, it is violations of institutional expectations that really get under the teacher's skin.[8]

In the reward system of the hidden curriculum, the student bears the cost of conforming to classroom custom in return for the prized benefit of teacher's praise.

It is not at all comforting to think that schools, through an unreflective use of this form of power, are creating a generation of graduates who may have learned that passive conformity—mindless consent and obedience, rather than informed agreement—pays off in school more often than active curiosity and aggressive imagination. If this is the case, schools are creating the basis of an extremely serious power problem. Imagination is disruptive in its very nature and spoils the prospects of passive conformity. A nation schooled to avoid the disruptions of imagination in favor of the quiet, meager benefits of adaptation for the sake of teacher's praise, is a nation about to lose its morality.

I should stress that not all imagination is valuable and not *all* obedience is a threat to morality; the implicit pattern of sacrificing imaginative thought for adaptive thoughtlessness is the real threat. There is a danger that we may come to believe that we are no longer capable of acting out of our own purposes, that we are capable of acting only as agents for fulfilling the plans of others. This is a mindless state of obedient isolation where responsibility has only technical but no social meaning, and where conscience is as rare as curiosity.

As in other forms of power, ultimate control in those relationships governed by finance lies in the presence and strength of consent. In classrooms, consent from the students comes out as a show of interest, as attention. Students *pay* attention. (For now, I want to pass by the fact that attendance at school is compulsory by law. What goes on at the school once everybody is present interests me more in these pages.)

The teacher has certain delegated powers that are not often at issue in the classroom, but whether this power can be turned into authority is another question. Power that is respected by those subject to it becomes authority precisely by virtue of that judgment. Students make that judgment by paying or withholding their attention. A teacher will expect, and some will demand, a show of respect from students precisely for this reason. The universal sign of such respect in a classroom is a payment of interest. Teachers know it, and students learn it fast.

"The possibility of massive inattention, signalling the loss of the teacher's authority, is frequently reported as a dominant fear among beginning teachers."[9] For the teacher, gaining the students' attention is an instrumental means for achieving some educational objective. For students, attention and inattention are the instruments of their claim to power in the classroom. Paying attention is a way of giving consent; the teacher's authority, and ultimately the teacher's power, are contingent on this consent. Teachers are well advised that boredom breeds inattention, and that boredom is the enemy of their power. The organized withdrawal of consent is the power over power in schools just as it is in other organizations.

The management of attention, then, becomes a central power issue in teaching. The fear of widespread inattention goes some way in explaining many teachers' preoccupation (enchantment?) with rules for classroom operations and etiquette. Some students may succeed in manipulating the reward system of the schools by learning to fake, flout, or flaunt their selective payments of attention, depending on the costs of the situation and their needs for reward.

In broad terms, the bargain struck in the classroom is an exchange of attentiveness (at least the appearance of attentiveness), or involvement, for the teacher's positive evaluation. The costs are slight for some students because their plans do not seriously conflict with the teacher's plans, but others pay a much higher price by losing their sense of curiosity, individuality, and social responsibility in a glaze of thoughtless, obedient fulfillment of someone else's expectations.

In this form of power, as in the fiction form, the teacher's point is to get students as individuals, and as whole classes, to develop a commitment to a particular educational activity. The educational purpose of the exchange of reward for services is to attract attention, develop interest, cultivate involvement, and crown the effort with a witting, voluntary, wholehearted commitment to something worth the price of that effort.

Fealty.   Fealty (faithfulness or loyalty that is based on trust and mutuality) is close to love, and love is commonly thought to be not at all like power. And yet if the analysis of power done so far is correct, fealty emerges as one of its most stable forms. I have argued that power is present in all social situations in which at least two people are related through a plan for action. The task in such power relations is to secure consent to the plan and cooperation in putting it into effect. We have seen how this can be done by force, storytelling, and the exchange of rewards for services. How else can it be done?

To answer this question, we must imagine two or more people who have the same plan, who share all information relevant to that plan, and who have achieved a balanced trust with each other. Consent is assumed and needs no management, no enforcement. All resources that would otherwise be used in such management and enforcement are freed to be directed at the plan itself. Time, energy, and attention can be concentrated on the tasks required by the plan, and not dissipated in suspicion and fear. The result is a remarkable stability in power relationships.

As power takes on forms that more and more closely approximate balanced trust, shared understanding, and a mutual plan for action, more and more of one's available resources are freed for application to the plan itself. Time, energy, and attention can be concentrated on the tasks required by the plan, and not dissipated in suspicion and fear. The kind of human organization that achieves these characteristics, whether between two people or among many, is imbued by something close to what we call the power of love. It is just here that power and love begin to merge in fealty as the most stable of all social schemes: reciprocal, cooperative commitment.

At this point in power theory, or in educational philosophy, one is often tempted to commit a common fallacy, to say that when a relationship achieves a condition of balanced trust, shared understanding, and a mutual plan for action, we are talking about something other than power. I would argue that, in fact, we are talking about the highest form of power in a relationship that contains all of the necessary basic conditions in their most stable conformation. The moralistic fallacy of insisting that we cannot think of love and power as appropriate descriptors of the same thing is detrimental to an understanding of both power and love. It is exactly our baneful enchantment with this illogic which must be overpowered.

When we understand power as an aspect of any social transaction that involves delegation, consent, and effect, we see that the key to long-term success lies in the informed goodwill of the consenter. As consent approaches complete willingness, based on informed judgment and invigorated by a personal motivation to accomplish the plan in question, then delegation and consent mingle into a sort of mutual cooperation that requires no vigilance, coercion, or force. Since all of the collective resources available through the relationship can be applied directly to accomplishing the plan, this form of power is highly efficient. As a description of effective cooperation this form of power could apply equally well to a revolutionary army, a law firm, a hockey club, a trapeze act, a class project, or a marriage.

In the literature of modern educational theory, Carl Rogers comes closest to espousing this view. A brief and somewhat crude summary of Rogers' position is that (1) teaching is a vastly overrated function; (2) the goal for education ought to be the facilitation of learning; and (3) the qualities of a good learning facilitator are "realness" as a person, a predominant attitude of "prizing, acceptance, and trust," an ability for "empathetic understanding," and a "profound trust in the human organism and its potentialities."[10] Success for Rogers is the creation of a sensitive climate of trust and understanding in which individuals can work together with a sense of community.

But Rogers' vision remains incomplete because he, like most other educational theorists, does not see this facilitation as a culmination of refined power principles. Instead, he sees his person-centered approach to social relations in education as disjunctive with the idea of power, as is apparent from the chapter title "Power or Persons: Two Trends in Education," in his recent book.[11] Rogers' program confronts the problem of trust between persons head on, using this direct focus to "facilitate" the creation of a climate in which "inner strength" can develop into "personal power."

The outcomes of such a program vary, but a fairly constant and characteristic result is an invigorated flush of initiative and self-interest, a sense that is too often flattened and matted by the constant pressure of organizational life. While I have no doubts that this experience is in many regards desirable, Rogers' program does not address the basic problems of power in its several forms. It tends, instead, to revert to a wholly psychological interpretation of power as a mixed set of personal attitudes, traits, and abilities. I also suspect that there may be a parallel between Rogers' program and the hedonist's paradox. A hedonist believes that pleasure brings happiness, and so seeks pleasure directly. After a lifetime of pleasure-seeking, the hedonist is surprised to find little satisfaction in old age, and therefore, less happiness than he had anticipated. Others who have given much of themselves to their work, who have loved as unselfishly as they could, who have accomplished things at considerable sacrifice to pleasure per se sense great happiness in their lives. Paradoxically, those who do not seek pleasure directly may well find more of it than those who do.

And so it may be with fealty as a form of power. That it is a form of power, I have no doubt. I have less confidence that a group can set out to achieve it for the purpose of gaining happiness or power. It seems more likely that it would occur as a consequence of, or even along with, another form of power.

In the context of this analysis of power it becomes possible to see the split between behaviorism and humanistic psychology, between B. F. Skinner and Carl Rogers, in a slightly different way. These two views represent different conceptions of power and not a total theoretical opposition. Skinner's ideal of a behavior-centered relationship based on perfectly managed contingencies of reinforcement is a representation of the financial form of power. Rogers' ideal of a relationship that is deeply meaningful, sensitive to the requirements of respect, and person-centered is a representation of the fealty form. Neither is a very realistic appraisal of power relations, but each has something to contribute to an understanding of power in educational theory.

Conflict, Authority, and Consent

Starting with the question of why power does not appear in the lexicon of educators, even though it is a fundamental concept in human experience, I have argued that, ever since Plato's *Gorgias,* education has been thought of as a symbol for virtue and placed in polar opposition to power, the symbol of evil. This expurgation of power from philosophy of education has helped to produce the American tendency to equate power with force, and therefore to see it as a perpetual enemy of love.

The redintegration of power in educational philosophy first requires our recognition that there are three forms of power relations which are more complex and refined than the mere use of force. Fiction, finance, and fealty are each forms of power that are theoretically compatible with educational purposes and processes. This is not to say that *every* manifestation of each form would be harmonious with educational goals. For instance, a certain kind of educational story whose plot is the deliberate limitation of thought and the non-rational control of belief is called indoctrination, and it has no place in education. The point is, however, that at least in some of their manifestations, these forms of power are not only compatible with education, but belong to its very essence.

Any consideration of the practice of power in education leads to a consideration of conflict, a concept that many see as intrinsic to power, and one that most educators would like to see legislated out of existence. Next to inattention the teacher fears conflict in the classroom more than anything else. Perhaps some teachers would put conflict first and inattention second, but the important point is that these two fears often go together. Inattention leads to disruption and conflict; but disruption and conflict can lead to inattention, too.

The elaborate system of rules and institutional expectations for the management of conflict which is characteristic of schools is possibly the single most important source of socialization that students will ever meet. These rules and their enforcement become associated with the organization itself and with the roles that one assumes within it, rather than with particular people. Individual teachers may change from hour to hour, year to year, and at any time substitutes may be brought in, but always *a* teacher has the delegated power to control conflict by enforcing rules and expectations. As noted earlier, violations of these rules and of institutional expectations upset teachers more than their students' intellectual failures. This reaction is a consequence of the view that conflict is intrinsic to power, that all power involves conflict. Given the vestigial assumption that power does not belong in education, and that conflict is intrinsic to power, teachers conclude that a sign of conflict is a sign of a power problem creeping in where none should be. Conflict, therefore, is not to be tolerated.

(There has always been the exceptional teacher who recognizes the creative tension that conflict can produce, and who uses that tension for really significant effects. But the conscious and deliberate use of conflict as a pedagogical means is not common.)

There is an important distinction to be made, however, between conflict and power. The wish to avoid conflict in schools, whether for practical reasons in a class of forty-five, or for psychological reasons of a more personal nature, must not be confused with a similar wish to avoid power relations, or power talk. Conflict is characteristic only of some power relations; it is not inherent in the idea of power. One reason that educators avoid talk of power in their own work is that they wish to avoid talk of conflict, and they hold the mistaken belief that all power involves conflict.

Conflict implies more than a difference between people, it implies a hostile encounter, struggle and resistance. The use of force is a frequent result (and source) of conflict, to be sure. And force *is* a form of power. But I have argued that the critical link in power relationships is consent; that consent can be described as a continuum of attitudes and actions from acquiescence under threat, to commitment through informed judgment; and that there are different forms of power (fiction, finance, and fealty) that operate with consent of one sort or another, but without force. It is therefore quite sensible to talk about power in education without assuming that conflict must produce it, or that power must produce conflict.

A few people in this world have a charismatic gift for eliciting commitment to a principle and organizing efforts to act on that principle. No one quite understands how this phenomenon works, but it would seem that such charismatic leaders are at least good storytellers. Political parties look for (but seldom find) candidates who will attract a following by telling good platform stories. Gandhi became the embodiment of consensus through his spiritual voice. It is quite possible to imagine a student leader who is able to lead by representing an agreement among those who want to be led, and not by virtue of a successful battle in a hostile conflict within the group. If such a person is able to coordinate effective, cooperative action, then that person is exercising power without conflict as a necessary antecedent or consequence. In fact, preventing conflict from developing, or controlling the agenda, is an effective form of power.[12]

Teachers are expected to be good motivators. They are told that motivation is an important problem, and that if students are not motivated they will not learn. In my way of thinking, motivating someone is just getting him to do something that he otherwise might not do on his own. Stated in terms that are familiar by now, to motivate is to enlist the consent of another person for carrying out one's plan for action. By motivating a student to learn something, a teacher is exercising power in almost paradigmatic fashion. And no conflict is necessarily involved.

A student may be listless, or distracted, or just generally anxious about undertaking anything alone. If a teacher can inspire such a student to investigate a problem—by overcoming indifference or anxiety rather than by overcoming hostile conflict—then, in the very act of motivating, the teacher has exercised power. One person (teacher) is related to another (student) through a plan for action (curriculum, project) in producing an instrumental effect (investigation). That is a power relationship which does not involve any hostile encounter, struggle and resistance; it does not involve conflict.

The teacher could accomplish this feat using any of the three forms of power presented in the preceding section. The teacher could tell a story ("Your work has shown me that you have a splendid talent for this sort of investigating, and I think you could be the best in the class if you only tried"); or strike a bargain ("If you get to work on this right now, I'll let you feed the gerbils after lunch"); or work with the student in a frame of balanced cooperation ("Here, I'll tell you what I know about this problem and then we'll figure out what to do next").

In the language of education, then, motivation is frequently a euphemism for power. Even if power had not been formally expurgated from the philosophy of education, educators would be unlikely, as indeed most others are, to talk directly about power in their own work because to do so requires that one talk about powerlessness, too, and that can be very depressing—especially for teachers. Consequently, talk about power in education tends to be mostly ceremonial and very grand: "There is no power on earth to compare with the power of education"; "Knowledge is power"; "Education is the engine of social change"; and so on.

On the practical level teachers are trained to think of their own power as a "last resort," a weapon whose use is a sign of one's failure to establish authority, discipline, order, and a proper motivation for achievement. But this sort of distinction is a sign of a double standard, for each of the items in the list of "failures" is an actual or potential aspect of power, not its contrary. Bertrand Russell summed up this particular sort of fallacy with laconic wit: "I am firm; you are stubborn; he is pigheaded." In the same vein: I inspire; you motivate; he resorts to power.

To speak of power, except as the last resort of a poor teacher, is to violate an informal normative rule as to the language of educational studies. As Dan Lortie has pointed out in his study of schoolteachers, "The traditions of teaching make people who seek money, prestige, or power somewhat suspect; the characteristic style in public education is to mute personal ambition."[13] Lortie is expressing the view of power held by the teachers in his study. For them power, whatever it means, is suspect; and people who are interested in it, and talk about it in terms of their own work, are suspect too. Any claim to power which would not violate these conventions must be expressed as specifically delegated authority over students. The teacher may prize this delegated authority, but no teacher is "supposed to *enjoy* exercising power per se."[14] In an education context, power is treated as such a thing to be compared with venal self-indulgence.

A passage from *Ethics and Education,* R. S. Peters' widely read and much admired text, shows how pointedly these rules of language are set out, and illustrates the disdain with which power is still treated in philosophy of education:

> "Authority" is most in evidence in the sphere of social control where we have authority systems; we speak of those "in authority" or "the authorities." In this sphere it must be distinguished from power with which it is too often confused by political theorists and sociologists alike. "Power" basically denotes ways in which an individual subjects others to his will by means of physical coercion (e.g., infliction of pain, restriction of movement), or by psychological coercion (e.g., withholding food, water, shelter, or access to means of attaining such necessities), or by the use of less dire forms of sanction and rewards (e.g., by manipulating access to material resources and rewards, sexual satisfaction, etc.), or by personal influences such as hypnotism or sexual attraction. Authority, on the other hand, involves the appeal to an impersonal normative order or value system which regulates behavior basically because of acceptance of it on the part of those who comply.[15]

Who, having read this passage, would dare look such a vile and detestable concept in the eye and still expect to be thought fit to teach? But the pitfalls of this expurgatory way of thinking about power should now be apparent.

As we move along the continuum of consent to the point at which those who give their consent give it willingly (and perhaps even with informed judgment), then, according to Peters, we are no longer talking about power. At that point we give the relationship another name that sounds more legitimate, and in the act of renaming we unwisely beguile ourselves into believing that the essential character of power has been replaced by a willing consent to a normative order that regulates behavior on the basis of this consent. We foolishly think that power has been purified by baptism as "authority," that power itself no longer exists in the new consecration. But Simon who is now called Peter is just Simon with another name, and authority is a type of power, not something altogether different. Authority is simply power that is respectable, or acceptable, to those who delegate it in the first place and who then consent to it. Authority remains just as vulnerable to the withdrawal of consent as other kinds of power. All power is contingent on consent; authority is contingent on respect in addition to consent.

Most teachers know the feeling of powerlessness which comes when students refuse to respect their claims to authority and the value system on which the claims are based. This feeling can lead a desperate teacher to conclude that force is the only means of restoring authority. But power takes many forms between authority and force, and teachers must become aware that they have alternatives and need not resort to force when their claims to authority are challenged—as they always have been and always will be. Force begets violence. If a better understanding of power can prevent resorting to force, then it can prevent violence, too.

Conclusion

The key to understanding power is the concept of consent. Consent holds power together. The continuum worked out in Chapter 2 identified five types of consent, or five phases in the development of consent. These are: (1) acquiescence under threat of sanction, (2) compliance based on partial or slanted information, (3) indifference due to habit or apathy, (4) conformity to custom, and (5) commitment through informed judgment.

Few would dispute the statement that a sense of purposefulness tends to strengthen consent. If a person knows what is being asked and why it is required, and if that person uses this information to develop a sense of purpose about what must be done, then that person will approach commitment, which is the strongest type of consent known. Through the mind to the heart is the path to power. People who are treated as if they do not matter, or as if it does not matter whether they understand what they are expected to do, are people who will react by tending toward withdrawal from, or confrontation with, the delegators. Withdrawal and confrontation are breaches between delegation and consent; each can destroy a power relation.

Purposefulness, which is the telling quality of consent in its highest stages of development, is a matter of having information, achieving understanding, and making judgments. It is here that education provides the link between the ideals of democratic designs for governing social relations and the ideals of power. The ideal citizen in a democracy is one who is able to consent or dissent on the basis of educated judgment, that is, on the basis of adequate information, well understood, and used for moral ends. In power theory, the ideal is to achieve the most stable form of cooperative efforts in accomplishing a plan. Both the ideal educated democratic citizen and the individuals in an ideal power relationship require the same things for consent of a purposeful nature—information, understanding, and judgment—and the provision of these is the ideal aim of education.

Education is the instrument of democratic designs. And it is no less the instrument of power. The control of information, the shaping of understanding, and the influence of judgment are critical elements common to democratic design, power theory, and educational philosophy. For achieving the purposes of democratic interests and for the realization of stable, durable power relationships, education has the instrumental task of moving students along the continuum of consent as far from acquiescence and as close to commitment through informed judgment as it is possible to do.

Consent of this type (commitment through informed judgment) is both a power ideal, and a democratic ideal. It is a power ideal because it is the most stable and efficient form that power can take. It is a democratic ideal because it is the basis of purposeful participation in cooperative government. Developing a capacity for rational commitment among as many people as it can is the first purpose of education in a democracy where the wide distribution of power is a moral imperative.

Part II

THE PROBLEM
OF FREEDOM

In Chapter 5 I hope to show how freedom can be understood as a corollary of power, and how the skills of acting freely can be taught. Chapter 4 introduces this argument by establishing a context of current views of freedom, examining their limits, and emphasizing the ambiguous nature of the concept itself. Since power plays no role in these views of freedom, there is little reference to it. For this reason, Chapter 4 stands in contrast to the rest of the book and illustrates what happens to freedom when it is put in a relation of polarity with power.

4 /

"Lyberte or Freedome Is a Mouche Swete Thynge"[1]

The great name of freedom stands for an idea, the objective reality of which is itself questionable. The influence of this idea, objectively real or not, has been enormous, as all of our recorded histories testify. This fact should teach us to have a deep respect for the practical effects of philosophical abstractions. Ideas like freedom can be life-giving or quite literally lethal. Freedom is an idea that can draw blood.

The application of freedom to education has caused, and will continue to cause, serious theoretical and public divisions, given that it is logically, morally, and practically impossible to approve all freedoms or all forms of education. In spite of their ambivalent relations to the concept of power, however, Americans—and in particular American educators—seem absolutely charmed by the concept of freedom. The two concepts stand in a somewhat paradoxical relationship: we expurgate power from our vocabulary, never stop chattering about freedom, but do not know what either one means—despite the fact that they are inherent in everything we do.

I hope it is clear at the end of this chapter—by implication if not by explication—that the idea of power has not guided educators in thinking about freedom. In the next chapter I will propose a revised logic of freedom that is guided by power theory, that is teachable, and that is meant to be of practical use for those who must make policy in educational matters, and in other social contexts that demand considerations of, and appeals to freedom in rendering just solutions to problems of many kinds. My purpose is to demonstrate the essential place of freedom in educational theory and to make it less elusive as a practical principle that can and should inform educational judgment.

The Structural Ambiguity of Freedom

I. A. Richards has written that all of our most important words are systematically ambiguous.[2] Words such as "free" and "education," among many others, qualify as our most important for two reasons: (1) "They cover the ideas we can least avoid using, those which are concerned in all that we do as thinking beings"; and (2) "They are words we are forced to use in explaining other words because it is in terms of the ideas they cover that the meaning of other words must be given." Richards went on to say that in general "we find that the more important a word is, and the more central and necessary its meanings are in our pictures of ourselves and the world, the more ambiguous and possibly deceiving the word will be. Naturally these words are also those which have been most used in philosophy."[3]

Our whole recorded history openly attests to the pliable resourcefulness of freedom, a word that has been invoked to serve endless purposes. It is one of the most important words in our language, not so much because it helps to resolve disputes or solve intricate dilemmas, but because to consider it and its diversity of meanings is inevitably to learn something more about civilized human life and values. "Freedom" stands for ideas that we cannot do without, albeit ambiguous ideas that have survived the persistent efforts of philosophers, poets, and politicians to reduce them to a single universal definition.

We sometimes think of freedom as a basic human condition, as a specific legal or political status, or as a psychological trait (as in "free spirit," or "free and easy fellow"). We tend to treat freedom as "a thing which a person may 'have' or 'possess' like a stamp collection or a headache."[4] This tendency reflects the fact that in philosophy, political theory, and psychology—the three main disciplines that offer literatures of freedom—there is a shared conception, and possibly a serious misconception, of freedom—as a noun. In treating freedom as a noun, however, we run the risk of reifying it and indenturing ourselves to it just as we have done with other abstractions, such as "life," "happiness," "growth," or "truth." Once we have bound ourselves to such abstractions, it becomes easy to justify foolish and even wicked things with principles that are taken to be reverentially pure.

A good example of this conundrum is John Stuart Mill's well-known insistence that "over himself, over his own body and mind, the individual is sovereign."[5] This statement represents perhaps the most ancient source of the idea of liberty, namely, the idea of privacy. Some maintain that John Stuart Mill was motivated to write the statement I quoted and the book I quoted from by the "fact that he thought it his own business whether or not he wanted to live with his mate out of marriage. He did just this and people were scandalized."[6] Against these circumstances, Mill's claim means one thing, but against the circumstances of the unfettered economic individualism of nineteenth-century England, of the unrestricted *laissez-faire* capitalism that destroyed children in the mines and mills and condemned the surviving parents to lives of sorrow, ignorance, and odious poverty, it means quite another. These contrasting circumstances stand for two very different approaches to the assessment of individual liberty, and when taken together, they illustrate the deep ambiguity of the concept.

Of course, caution is required in appealing to historical uses of "freedom," for the meaning of the term is partly the meaning of the times in which it was used. In the United States between 1787 and 1947, for instance, a transformation took place from freedom as natural rights (rights *against* the government, rights of independence), to civil liberties (rights to *participate* in civil government), to human freedoms (rights to the *help* of government in achieving protection from fear and want). The Declaration of Human Rights of 1949 included a dimension of freedom which encompasses the development of creativity, or the ability to develop one's essential human capacities. "This dimension of freedom calls for social security, for work, for education, and rest. It requires a rich cultural life and internal order."[7]

"Freedom in modern America depends less than ever before on resistance to the controls exerted by others and more than ever on (a person's) own willpower and self-control. External vigilance remains the price of liberty, but the first person to watch is oneself."[8] This vision leads the historian David Potter to the profound notion that

> if power and control are something more than the application of force, then freedom must consist of something more than immunity from the application of force. . . . A broader definition would take into account the limitations of freedom achieved by the exploitation of needs. In such terms, the principal diagnostic feature of freedom might well be a condition in which needs are either reduced to a minimum or somehow rendered unexploitable. To construe freedom in this way is to recommend a fundamental reworking of the whole history of freedom in America—a history usually written as a record of the restraints placed on coercive power.[9]

Most people assume that most people want more freedom. But this is not obviously true. Desire for status, understanding, and a common dependence with others is not the same as a desire for increased freedom. Some demands for freedom, on the other hand, are disguised demands for power; in fact power and freedom are closely related through the core idea of being able to act according to intention. Each time a person is empowered with new freedom(s), that person is required to make many new and often difficult decisions, and to be responsible for the decisions taken. (*Liberté*, as it was used in the eighteenth century, strongly implied responsibility.) My experience is that many people (including me, sometimes) are glad to leave a number of these decisions to others and thereby avoid responsibility. In maximizing freedom one does not always (or even often) maximize happiness. It is probably true, as Dostoyevsky's Grand Inquisitor insisted, that, given a choice, most people will prefer happiness to freedom. Other values, such as security, peacefulness, and intimate association, compete with freedom more often than they complement it.

But as Locke never tired of insisting, the concentration of power is the death of freedom, and it is precisely those without power who feel the least (politically, and socially) free. On the subject of "feeling free," Felix Oppenheim reminds us that there is

> nothing paradoxical about the fact that well-indoctrinated members of an Orwellian society feel free even though they are officially unfree in almost every respect. It is in this connection that the distinction between freedom as an objective relation between actors and freedom as a subjective state of mind becomes especially important.[10]

Having a freedom is not always a pleasant state: for example, having no obligations and "nothing to do" drives some people into misery and madness. I think that the pleasantness, or desirability of certain freedoms is related to the idea of relevance, in one of its two senses: either (1) as a means-to-end relation; or (2) as a whole-part coherence. One would tend to feel free and like the feeling when one is conscious of an ability to act in accord with values thought to be relevant to one's life purposes; and one would feel either unfree, or disagreeably free when acting in accord with non-relevant values or without any conscious values. I think one can conclude that to feel free is not necessarily the same as to be able to act freely, and to be able to act freely is not necessarily to feel free or to be happy about it.

The fact that freedom is a universal concept contributes to its ambiguity, for, since everyone may presume to speak from personal experience with freedom (and most everyone does), its nature is confused by conflicting authorities. The outcome is a jumble of qualities and values which yields not a clear definition but only an elusive state of mind, like being tired, contented, or sexually satisfied. The unmanaged range of things that the terms "freedom" and "liberty" have come to represent, and the noticeable lack of progress we have made in sorting out our confusions about this range of things, should make us question the quality of our thinking on these matters, and the habits we may have fallen into when thinking about them.

The Essential Contestability of Freedom

Some would argue that the characteristic ambiguity of freedom is evidence that its worth as a concept has been overestimated. They would say that since its "real meaning" eludes analysis, it is a meaningless concept and we shouldn't bother with it. But this logic would lead one to a similar conclusion about justice, art, education, progress, and goodness, just to mention a few examples.

But this introduction to the difficulties of the idea of freedom should not be read as praise for ambiguity itself. Ambiguity is no more a "good" than is precision; these are aspects of language, not virtues (notwithstanding Bertrand Russell's remark that the demand for certainty is natural to man, but is nevertheless an intellectual vice).

It is absurd to argue that, lacking certainty, there are no standards by which choices and various meanings can be assessed with respect to their relative and potential worth for solving problems in particular contexts. The fact that several legitimate and incompatible meanings can exist for a concept such as freedom does not warrant the conclusion that the several meanings are therefore either meaningless or equally meaningful. Unlike Shakespeare's claim for love ("Love is not love that alters when it alteration finds"), meaning is established and refined in use, and it does alter as circumstances change, and as new contexts come about.

Freedom is an essentially contestable concept in W. B. Gallie's sense of essential contestability.[11] Gallie shows that there are disputes about certain concepts that cannot be resolved by argument of any kind; that is to say, there are concepts "the proper use of which inevitably involves endless disputes about their proper uses on the part of their users."[12] Gallie outlines four conditions that a concept must possess if it is to count as essentially contested.

> (I) It must be *appraisive* in the sense that it signifies or accredits some kind of valued achievement. (II) This achievement must be of an internally complex character, for all that its worth is attributed to it as a whole. (III) Any explanation of its worth must therefore include reference to the respective contributions of its various parts or features; yet prior to experimentation there is nothing absurd or contradictory in any one of a number of possible rival descriptions of its total worth, one such description setting its component parts or features in one order of importance, a second setting them in a second order, and so on. In fine, the accredited achievement is *initially* variously describable. (IV) The accredited achievement must be of a kind that admits of considerable modification in the light of changing circumstances; and such modification cannot be prescribed or predicted in advance.[13]

Although concepts that manifest these conditions are likely to persist in vagueness and ambiguity, it remains important to scrutinize their various uses in order to ascertain different degrees of logical force and justifiability. Disputes that are carried on at the emotional-ideological level may well fail to take account of the nature of the disputed concept and therefore fail to make progress toward understanding the concept.

> Recognition of a given concept as essentially contested implies recognition of rival uses of it (such as oneself repudiates) as not

only logically possible and humanly 'likely', but as of permanent potential critical value to one's own use or interpretation of the concept in question; whereas to regard any rival use as anathema, perverse, bestial or lunatic means, in many cases, to submit one-self to the chronic human peril of underestimating the value of one's opponent's positions.[14]

Freedom, as an appraisive, internally complex concept whose various parts and features produce rival descriptions of its total worth—descriptions that are neither absurd nor con-tradictory—counts as essentially contestable. Its accredited achievement is of a kind that admits of modification as cir-cumstances change, and disputes about freedom in educational theory are therefore respectable when freedom is recognized as essentially contestable. In the remainder of the chapter I will discuss the internal complexity and three rival descrip-tions of freedom to see what logical force they possess for educational theory.

Rival Meanings of Freedom

Those who think that all meanings of freedom are equal think so on the premise that meanings are basically subjective constructs and liable only to personal assessment, i.e., any-body's chosen meaning is as good (as "valid") as anybody else's. This view is untenable for several reasons. Aside from the ob-vious reminder that "equal" is another of our most important words, and that its own ambiguities must be observed before it can be invoked to defend the subjective construct view of "free-dom" and of meaning in general, there is a more generic objec-tion. This objection has two parts: (1) the value of a meaning of freedom cannot be justified without appeal to other values, and the meaning of these other values may or may not be consis-tent with a given meaning of freedom; (2) it is not possible to endorse all meanings of freedom, all freedoms, without con-tradiction.

The argument for the first part of the objection is roughly

this: If A claims that freedom means "whatever one can do and wants to do, one may do," and that this meaning of freedom is equal with any other, then A must answer B's challenge that for him (B) freedom means "whatever one can do and wants to do, one may do, except if it causes pain to anyone else," and that what A proposes to do (e.g., burn B's manuscript to keep warm) will cause B pain; therefore, A is not free to do as he can and wishes to do. If these meanings of freedom are equal and conflicting, we have a dilemma: both A and B are restricted by the other's view of freedom. A is prohibited by B from burning B's manuscript on the ground it would interfere with both A's and B's conception of freedom (B can and wants to protect his manuscript, so he may protect it; B also claims that if A exercises his freedom it would cause B pain). B is restricted in a slightly different way; he is forced to be vigilant of his manuscript so that A won't get a chance to burn it, and this diverts his attention from other matters. The dilemma remains unresolved until an appeal is made to another value, which could be any one of several (respect for private property, compromise, friendship, censorship, or the communal authority of civil law). In this example, B's meaning of freedom is more consistent with an appeal to another value, because of its conditional clause, and therefore might be considered a "better" meaning so long as the resolution of conflicts over freedom is also held to be a value. It should be noted in conclusion that some other value must be held for freedom itself to be of any value. Calling the ideal of freedom "good," or "humane," or "democratic" is only to put off the question, "For what?" And when that question is answered, the basis for assigning value to a meaning of freedom will have been laid, or mislaid, depending on whether the meanings are shown to be compatible. (If the answer to the question "For what?" is "nothing," then what would be lost without freedom? If the answer to that question is also "nothing," freedom is neither gain nor loss; it has no apparent value.)

The argument for the second part of the objection to the

subjective construct view, namely, that one cannot endorse all meanings of freedom, all freedoms, without contradiction, can be elucidated in a single example. If all freedoms are allowed, A is free to arrogate B's freedoms, even to take B's life. If to give A all freedoms is to make a slave of B, and if slavery is taken to meen unfreedom, then to endorse all freedoms is to endorse unfreedom as well; both justified under the same principle. It takes considerable guile and dexterity even to attempt a defense of such a position.

Freedom is a swete thynge, but it is a complex thing, too. Many persons have died for it, killed for it, some long for it while others fear it, some have been awarded government grants to figure out how to keep it for allies and take it away from enemies, who are often defined in terms of how they define freedom and what they are willing to do to get it and keep it. It is important to continue trying to understand the idea of freedom, because the idea is crucial to human life. No less important is the idea of education, and no less ambiguous, as any one concerned with understanding the controversy over the reappearance of free schools is bound to judge.

Freedom and Free Schools

"A foolish consistency is the hobgoblin of little minds, adored by little statesmen and philosophers and divines. With consistency a great soul has simply nothing to do."[15] Emerson goes on in "Self-Reliance," this most celebrated of his essays, to pick at the intellectual glue of the arguments just presented, namely that thinking of freedom in relation to other values is worthy and best done with respect both for the structural ambiguity of our most important words, and for consistency in reasoning. In his tribute to individualism and non-conformity, Emerson foreshadows the spirit of the free schools that would follow him by more than a century:

> Society everywhere is in conspiracy against the manhood of every one of its members. . . . Whoso would be a man, must be a non-

conformist. . . . Nothing is at last sacred to me but that of my nature. Good and bad are but names very readily transferable to that or this; the only right is what is after my constitution, the only wrong what is against it. . . . Life only avails, not the having lived. Power ceases in the instant of respose; it resides in the moment of transition from a past to a new state, in the shooting of the gulf, in the darting of an aim.[16]

These snippets of Emerson are used as a beginning for a discussion of freedom and schooling, and of free schools in particular, because of their sententiousness, and because they echo modern exponents of educational freedom such as Jonathan Kozol, Paul Goodman, and Carl Rogers, whose works are cited below as evidence that while the issues and convictions haven't changed much, our progress toward their elucidation has been slow.

The character of the debate over free schools is often marred by a tendency to bifurcate complex issues. One is reminded of Dr. Johnson's imperious judgment on freedom: "Sir, we know our will is free, and there's an end on't."[17] Dr. Johnson says the will is free, while others—B. F. Skinner,[18] for example—stand just as firmly for the opposite view, that the will is not free and there's the *real* end on't. The alternatives left us by the contemporary proponents of free schools in many ways resemble these two bullish and opposing beliefs. One either opts for "love and freedom" and learns to believe that no learning can take place unless the pupil's environment is loving and free, or one feels pressure to say that learning is most likely to occur not when the pupil is free, but instead when he is well disciplined and diligent, loved or not. These alternatives are based on the view that "fear and authoritarianism" are the necessary alternatives of "love and freedom." In addition, it is widely assumed that no right-thinking, warm-blooded adult educator could still make policy on grounds of "fear and authoritarianism"; after all, the diastrous results of such policy are embarrassingly apparent in our crowds of conditioned consumers, our behemoth bureaucracies, our bellicose nationalism, our chauvinistic social constructs, and our sundry asylums. These alternatives are simplistic and based on a misunderstanding of freedom. The controversy over the place of freedom in education could be much improved by an appreciation of the complex reasoning that sustains it, and of the structural ambiguities that confuse it.

An unusually motley combination of appealing principles and stupefying practices has confounded the policy questions of free schools, and open education in general. One is as naturally drawn to most general principles of freedom as one is drawn to uncontaminated air. One is "for" them, but they are hardly thought of until they are taken away, or slip, during the night, out of our control. (But who ever worried about controlling fresh air until recently?) On the other hand, when certain principles of freedom are used in defining and endorsing educational policy in schools, especially free schools, awesome things occur.

In one free school I know of, the cooperative board of directors voted to allow the pupils freedom in using any means they wished for settling disputes that arose during the course of a free schoolday. The vote was not unanimous, but the policy was adopted, and in a few weeks the directors found themselves disagreeing over the issue of violence among the pupils.

Some of the directors argued for the cathartic benefits of freely expressed aggressions, and others argued that such individual therapy came at too high a price, that it was not in the community's better interests, that the long-term effects of such unruly and careless behavior would be destructive to the school's reputation and to the learned values of cooperation and compassion which had been assumed to underlie the whole notion of free schools. After all, for bullies they had public schools.

This is a long-hand way of illustrating the familiar observation that "your freedom ends where my nose begins." When speaking of children, it is crucial to remember that important as the nose is, behind it lies a fragile self, and a damaged sense of self is not so easy to spot and mend as a bloodied nose. What counts as behavioral freedom for one may indirectly, through fear and persuasion, wreck the psychological freedom of another.

Now I will discuss the cases made by three well-known advocates of free schools to illustrate three major principles of freedom—principles that are appealed to, mistakenly I think, in debates over all kinds of school policy. The first principle, that freedom is the highest aim or goal of schooling, is an aspect of Jonathan Kozol's view that the function of free schools is the realization of the *end* of liberation.

Kozol, like many others, tries to define "free school" *contra* traditional school, or public school, assuming that the latter already has an adequate definition, especially as that definition concerns freedom. In fact one's notion of a traditional school depends directly on one's definitions of "education" and "freedom," and, given the difficulties we have had in overcoming the ambiguities of both of these concepts, one would expect agreement on the definition of a traditional school to come hard, if at all. Nevertheless, the assumption apparently prevails that "traditional" or "public" school is a standard referent.

In *Free Schools,* Kozol reasons that "Free School, as the opposite of public school, implies not one thing but ten million different possibilities."[19] However, this admission does not serve to caution its author from asserting with considerable certainty his own "true" definition of free school: "The true, moral, political and semantic derivation of 'Free School' lies in 'Freedom School.' It is to the liberation, to the vision and to the potency of the oppressed that any Free School worth its derivation and its photographs of Neill, Tolstoy or Eldridge Cleaver must, in the long run, be accountable."[20] A free school, then, is an organization dedicated to the *condition of liberation* (i.e., freedom) of the oppressed. Kozol further characterizes such a school as being outside the public education system, inside cities, outside white man's "counterculture," in direct contact with needs of the poor and dispossessed, as small as can be managed, and unpublicized.

Kozol's vision of the eventual condition of human liberation as the organizing principle of free schools contrasts with a second common emphasis on what is "free" about free schools, an emphasis that is, like Kozol's, primarily sociological. Paul Goodman believed that we can educate the young

> entirely in terms of their free choice, with no processing whatsoever. . . . It seems stupid to decide a priori what the young ought to know and then to try to motivate them instead of letting the initiative come from them and putting information and relevant equipment at their service. It is false to assert that this kind of freedom will not serve society's needs—at least those needs that should humanly be served; freedom is the only way toward authentic citizenship and real, rather than verbal, philosophy. Free choice is not random but responsive to real situations; both youth and adults live in a nature of things, a polity, an ongoing society, and it is these, in fact, that attract interest and channel need.[21]

Continuing his policy of nonencroachment, Goodman claims that

> voluntary adolescent choices are often random and foolish and usually transitory; but they are the likeliest ways of growing up reasonably. What is most essential is for the youth to see that he is taken seriously as a person rather than fitted into an institutional system.[22]

Goodman clearly believed that being "taken seriously as a person" means being given virtually unlimited free choice, at least in one's education. Goodman has switched the emphasis from the *end* of freedom, to the *means* of freedom employed for the ends of "authentic citizenship and real, rather than verbal, philosophy," as well as due service to society's needs. Living with such faith must have been invigorating.

A third principle of "freedom" in education has been

tirelessly written about by Carl Rogers. I quote from "The Meaning of Freedom," a section of a chapter called "Freedom and Commitment" in his book *Freedom to Learn:*

> The freedom that I am talking about is essentially an inner thing, something which exists in the living person quite aside from any of the outward choices of alternatives which we so often think of as constituting freedom.... It is the realization that "I can live myself, here and now, by my own choice." It is the quality of courage which enables a person to step into the uncertainty of the unknown as he chooses himself. It is the discovery of meaning from within oneself, meaning which comes from listening sensitively and openly to the complexities of what one is experiencing. It is the burden of being responsible for the self one chooses to be. It is the recognition of a person that he is an emerging process, not a static end product. The individual who is thus deeply and courageously thinking his own thoughts, becoming his own uniqueness, responsibly choosing himself, may be fortunate in having hundreds of objective outer alternatives from which to choose, or he may be unfortunate in having none. But his freedom exists regardless.[23]

And there's *another* end on't.

In the remainder of this chapter I will deal with the three issues raised by these excerpts: (1) freedom as a goal of schooling, (2) the implication that taking one seriously as a person means giving one unlimited choice in one's education, and (3) the reification of freedom.

Freedom as a Goal

"Oh, Lord, I want to be free, want to be free; Rainbow around my shoulder, wings on my feet." The words of this old song capture in simple grace the sense of freedom as a goal. But freedom as a goal, like a rainbow, is an image that inspires pots of gold. The inspiration is of more substance than the pots.

Kozol has spoken for the ambition of producing a condition of liberation as a result of free-school experience. The ambition is common among free-school theorists, but not all limit the conditions of liberation in quite the way Kozol does. Nonetheless, his position can serve as an example of the faulty reasoning behind the ambition itself. Kozol argues that a free school is an organization dedicated to the liberation of the oppressed. But it seems that in his view not all qualify as "the oppressed." In fact, Kozol accuses other free-school advocates (e.g., those who retreat from urban terror and degradation to the country and the copse, the sylvan communities devoted to spontaneous behavior and simple values) of "running away" to a "moral vacuum," and thus contributing to the oppression of those left behind in the cities; never mind what reasons or conditions were responsible for these people's need to escape urban life. Kozol uses an ugly simile to emphasize his view: "In my belief, an isolated upper-class rural Free School for the children of the white and rich within a land like the United States and in a time of torment such as 1972, is a great deal too much like a sandbox for the children of the SS Guards at Auschwitz."[24]

We have here in Kozol's words the grounds for questioning the reasoning behind freedom as a goal. If the condition of liberation, of freedom, is to be sought as a good, as a goal, one would assume that as a good, freedom would be a legitimate goal for everyone. But this is not the case for Kozol, who claims that the freedom some seek is immoral (like the freedom of the SS), or at least amoral (a vacuum). The problem is in defining "the oppressed" who need freedom. Kozol rightly and passionately points out that economic and racial oppression should not be tolerated, and abuses of this sort are what his free school is designed to fight. But what is to be done for the emotionally retarded of any economic or racial group, the academic "success" who is also helplessly hypochondriacal, the children of sadistic parents, the wives of wife-beaters? Are they not rightly considered oppressed and in need of "liberation" from their circumstances? It is not immediately clear why it is less moral, or even immoral, to attempt to free someone from neurotic constraints (e.g., authoritarian compulsions, xenophobia, excessive greed), than to attempt to liberate some-one from economic or racial constraints. In short, it seems that most of us feel that some groups deserve freedom more than others; some sandboxes become evil depending on who plays in them.

When we speak of freedom as a goal, we do not generally mean freedom as a universal and absolute goal. To be free to do absolutely as one likes is to be free to oppress, to murder, to degrade, to take freedom from others. This clearly is not what free-school theorists such as Kozol seek, yet they go on speaking in a way that leaves them open to this sort of criticism. Their real intent seems to be the remediation of abuses that result when a depressingly large number of politicians, land-lords, moneylenders, and others of that general ilk exercise freedoms at the expense of those who haven't the *power* to protect themselves. But the remedy is not merely a wider dis-tribution of freedom; it is power—power to fight other powers in order to gain the opportunity to do something else. "Liberat-ing" might mean "empowering," but this is not the same as "being free." As Arnold put it in *Culture and Anarchy:*

> What is freedom but machinery? . . . In our common notions and talk about freedom, we eminently show our idolatry of ma-chinery. Our prevalent notion is . . . that it is a most happy and important thing for a man merely to be able to do as he likes. On what he is to do when he is thus free to do as he likes, we do not lay so much stress.[25]

But we have trouble thinking of freedom as machinery. We act according to the general presumption that we must defend the right of people to do what they want in order to be happy. We are very protective of this right, as if convinced that it is the sole means to attain happiness. But, as the literature of aliena-tion has documented copiously, happiness does not necessarily follow from the possession of freedom, for gains in freedom are often purchased at the expense of other values generally as-sociated with happiness—values such as the security and the contentment of familiar, reliable companionship. It is simply not realistic, given our experience with social groups, to expect that the inherent good will and decency, let alone the intelligence and imagination of a particular group will ensure the freedom to do as each member wants. The urge to self-expression creates tension and must be suppressed when individual wants are in conflict, if the group is to remain stable and continue to exist.

The conditions in which freedom is desired need rules and a consistent order to protect against the inconsistency of individuals. In fact, the choice as we have it is not "for" or "against" freedom, but for certain constraints and against others. There is no such thing as a general, concrete condition of freedom, but there are concrete problems of what some people want to do in particular and what it is that hinders or prevents them. Constraints are inherent necessities in social life, and to speak of freedom as a general aim or goal does not make sense. It makes more sense, given Kozol's interest in liberation, to speak of increasing the capacity for successful power relations among those who are oppressed by unacceptable constraints.

The goal of general freedom is a false goal for educators. But the goal of acquiring due power for the disenfranchised to choose well and effectively for themselves is legitimate, as is the goal of influencing any student's ability to discriminate for worth and fairness among rival wants. This conclusion leads to the next issue raised by the free-school literature, namely that respect for another person necessitates giving him or her unlimited free choice in educational matters.

Freedom, Choice, and Respect for Persons

"We should deal with children as God deals with us, for He makes us happiest when He lets us grope our way in a pleasant illusion." Just about the time I let Goethe's words convince me, a little poem by J. P. Donleavy jangles in the back of my mind:

> At the rate
> The world
> Is going
> It will
> Be
> Poor old
> Everybody[26]

Does respect for students mean that we should let them grope away in their pleasant illusions; will this groping lead us to poor old everybody? This is a question of normative freedom, perhaps the central question of free-school policy, and of educational policy in general.

Goodman's belief that we can educate the young "entirely in terms of their free choice, with no processing whatsoever" is a belief that either (1) every student's reasoning is intrinsically as valid, useful, and moral as anyone else's, or that (2) students' reasoning is beside the point of educating. If one believes the former, then the next step is to believe that everyone's reasoning is just as valid, useful, and moral as anyone else's. This view denies that there is any criterion at all that we can agree on as a basis for objective verification, justification, or even consistency. But if this is the case, then the opposite is equally true, because we have no way to test either claim. So we run into the paradox of having to believe that A is both A and not-A, and not to fret over it, or to fret over it; whichever we like. It is both easy and difficult to argue against this claim. It is easy because there is an abundance of examples that show the claim false in spite of anyone's opionion to the contrary (e.g., the proper, *correct,* change for $5 on a $1 purchase is $4; New York *is* larger than Rhode Island; as of 1980 Richard Nixon is the *only* president in U.S. history to resign his office; ½ means the *same* as "one-half"). There are criteria for objective verification and justification that we can and do agree on, and consistency underlies them all. But it is at the same time difficult to argue against the subjective view of knowledge and the idiosyncratic view of reasoning because those who hold such views don't care about consistency in argument. They care instead about their rights to say and do what and how they please, to grope their way in their own pleasant illusions, just as we others grope our way in the illusion of consistency and the possibilities of objective justification.[27] John Gardner made the point well in *Grendel:* "All order, I've come to understand, is theoretical, unreal—a harmless, sensible, smiling mask men slide between the two great, dark realities, the self and the world—two snake pits."[28] If Gardner succeeds in making us understand his meaning through our common use of language, he in some measure succeeds also in making an argument against himself, for surely there is order in the very language he uses, insofar as we use it with mutual understanding.

It is equally indefensible to claim that reasoning is beside the point of educating, especially given the common free-school principle of educating the "whole child," for reasoning is a part, a significant part, of a person's integrity as a "whole" person. To ignore reasoning is to do mental mayhem, to commit a character amputation. And Goodman himself aims for "authentic citizenship" and "real philosophy" through education, neither of which is conceivable without highly developed reasoning. In fact, connecting the accomplishment of any aim at all with any preferred or necessary means is an act of reasoning in and of itself, so any policy for educating on purpose relies on reasoning from the start.

The spirit of this normative freedom survives such analysis, however (even if its literal sense fades a bit), because all of us *do* want students to make choices for themselves, and to be responsible for their educations to a large, and in the end, controlling degree. The problem is that we are reluctant to assume the authority in teaching them how to make choices when their own education is the subject. We have trouble holding in mind both the principle that freedom in choosing is a desirable end, and the principle that good choices do not happen spontaneously or by gift alone, but must be acquired by learning how to reason and to perceive accurately in various circumstances. We make the mistake of believing that the best way to achieve an increase in some sort of freedom, for example, in choosing well among alternatives, is by way of freedom itself, by way of noninterference on the adult's part. That freedom as a means leads to freedom as an end is a dubious formula, however.

The question of the role of adults in free-school education is still the subject of loud debate, but three conceptions of that role seem to exhaust the imaginations of the debaters; we can call these alternatives: Abdication and Non-interference, Love and Be Loved, and Environmental Design. The first alternative is weak because it is hypocritical, unreal; it denies participation in the natural and necessary relations between people who share the same physical space for so much time, ostensibly for the same purposes. The second is unclear because if "love" is meant as caring and being cared for, we are left with no way of evaluating the many different ways one can "care for" another. It does not take an unusual imagination to conceive the circumstance in which caring, or loving, means taking away certain freedoms. The third, Environmental Design, "providing a rich environment," is insufficient because all hinges on what the designers consider "rich." This last alternative is distressingly similar to the behaviorist response to questions of education, namely, contingency management, which can be an insidious infringement on freedom through its indirect coercion and structured limitation of access.

The role of adults in education, be it the free-school or more traditional kind, can be more clearly understood if the principle of planning is kept in mind. Education that focuses on the present or the immediate future, as defined by the impulsive and short-sighted interests of unconstrained students, is hardly an education that contributes explicitly to the future well-being of students. I think all teachers would agree that they have a responsibility to teach skills and attitudes that will be useful and enjoyable long after the student leaves school. These skills and attitudes have much to do with planning, thinking ahead, and taking responsibility for the consequences of one's actions. These are the characteristics of educated persons, and they require that the student develop an ability to regulate action and thought according to anticipated future conditions, not the conditions of the immediate present. This ability is not easy to learn, but it can be taught; I will return to it as a critical aspect of a revised logic of freedom.

The Reification of Freedom

"Philosophy is a battle against the bewitchment of our intelligence by means of language."[29] Reification, according to the *Oxford English Dictionary,* means "to convert mentally into a thing; to materialize," and it is about the same as to hypostatize, which means "to make into or treat as a substance." Freedom has been reified into a "thing" worth fighting for; it has been materialized as a condition that exists and deserves homage, as the "substance" of various forms of government, as the idol of humanism. This is a birthing phenomenon similar to that undergone by western religions. Feuerbach sums up his analysis of the mystery of religion in *The Essence of Christianity* by claiming that "man . . . projects his nature into objectivity, and then makes himself an object of concern for this new 'subject,' for this projection of his nature."[30] In this sense then, religion is man's alienation from himself. Marx appropriated Feuerbach's analysis and used it in developing a general theory of alienation. Marx's emphasis was on product alienation and the fetishism of commodities, or the conversion of product relations into entities, which he treated as the religion of daily life. Bertell Ollman in his commentary on Marx's theory of alienation, suggests further that "by attributing an independent life to the various forms of value, people succeed in transferring to them certain powers for regulating their own existence."[31] As these forms take on "existence" they influence the way we see and how we judge what we see.

The legacy of Feuerbach and Marx to our understanding of

the nature and process of reification is central to our analysis of the idolization of freedom. This sort of reification is an attempt to rescue a chosen value from the altering influence of context, from the ambiguity these values possess through the long process in which they generate and refine civilization. But such influence cannot be avoided; being in a context means being influenced, and just as one cannot escape context, so one cannot escape influence.

Rogers' assertion that freedom is an inner thing, that it "exists regardless" of contextual circumstances and "objective outer alternatives," is a reified distortion of the social and instrumental character of the value we call freedom. Freedoms are particular aspects of particular situations that people experience, and as such, freedoms must be understood in connection with the particular constraints that give definition to those situations.

If we are born into a community, we are not born free. Perhaps the most comprehensive and brief introduction to this condition of human life is Freud's *Civilization and Its Discontents*.[32] The principal thesis of this book is that civilization progresses as the individuals in a culture learn to trade their instinctual "happiness" for the security they need to live among others, both within and without their given community. One aspect of the security thus gained is freedom from the potential oppression of others' instinctual needs. Freud's analysis of the "happiness for security" bargain in civilization is useful in developing a perspective on the plural nature of freedoms, on the necessary conflict between two kinds of freedom—freedom-as-instinct-gratification versus freedom-as-security. Following the arguments made by both Feuerbach and Freud, one can try to overcome the habit of treating freedom as an entity and argue that education has a central role in developing freedoms. Education for freedoms is certainly conceivable as education for better trading, for self-governance, for the powers of discrimination among desired and desirable wants.

As I have suggested, the generic terms of freedom are "you"

and "me" and "us." Your freedom, my freedom, and our freedom may not be compatible: we cannot affirm them all without some appeal to another value that governs not Freedom, but particular freedom*s*. Because particular freedoms entail at least two persons and the context they share, the issues raised in discussing freedoms are inevitably ethical ones, involving the rights of each to be granted, taken, or denied. Adler summarizes this point well in *The Idea of Freedom:*

> If some tension between *self* and *other* is involved in any conception of freedom, then law plays one role when it represents a power alien to the self, and another when the self is able to make the law somehow its own or an expression of its power. In the first role, law is an obstacle to freedom; in the second, it is a source of freedom, or even part of its substance.[33]

Again, I repeat that there is no general issue of freedom, but there are many issues of particular freedoms. Freedom can be defined in terms of independence, power, autonomy, choice, doing what one wants, and so on. None is sufficient for defining the magnificent singular Freedom, but each can be useful in defining the more diminutive freedoms. In education, these diminutive freedoms do not lead to an abdication of instructional responsibilities on the grounds that presenting alternatives is enough for a teacher to do. To know of alternatives is not the same as having a choice, any more than to know of theoretical justifications for freedom(s) is the same as being free. What one does with one's knowledge, subjective or objective as it may be, is the more important indication of one's degree of freedom(s), of one's education, and most important, of one's values for conduct. Freedom is machinery that makes various modes of conduct more or less possible; it is not an Idol to which one appeals in a solemn invocation for happiness.

Those like Rogers, who would reify freedom, or, like Goodman, who would see educational constraints as disrespectful of persons, miss a very important point about the nature of institutions. It is a false proposition that education, like the law, becomes a constraining institution if it does not allow absolute individual freedom, and that we therefore must choose freedom over constraint on the basis of respect for persons. Institutions of all kinds are inherently constraining because they are organizations and because when people are related through organization, individual freedoms are subject to the rules (constraints) of that organization. The question is not whether education should constrain individual freedoms (it must), but what exactly is the relation between institutional constraint and individual freedoms which renders education *just*. Kozol, Goodman, and Rogers mistakenly understand all educational constraints to be oppressive. Some excessive and unjustified institutional constraints (e.g., racist policy) are certainly oppressive, but others (e.g., policies providing an equal opportunity for people to do a given thing) are the *remedy* of oppression.

5 /

The Skills of Freedom

The theory of freedom has a dreary past and has produced a modern disaster. The dreariness comes from the persistent regularity with which so many have asked the wrong questions about freedom based on the mistaken presumption that freedom is the sort of thing that people possess or do not possess *simpliciter*. The disaster is that we have become so enthralled by Freedom as a magnificent singular abstraction that we defeat the humane possibilities of daily community life.

Freedom is a structurally ambiguous, essentially contestable, but indispensable and enduring concept that has appeared in all its varied plumage over two millennia as a normative aspect of social and educational philosophy. We cannot do without some idea of freedom even if we hardly know what to do with it. Nor can we do without the concept of education, another ambiguous, contestable, indispensable, and enduring idea. Freedom and education cleave together as mated social values, but the forms they take are protean. And like Proteus they elude us by changing shape as we approach too near.

Since my concept of power's various aspects influences my thinking about freedom, the view of freedom developed in this chapter is distinct from the view expressed in most educational studies, although it is not unique in all other regards. Those aspects of power which are especially relevant to this view are: a particular combination of psychological, social, and instrumental characteristics; a requirement for imagining, for planning; an emphasis on the ability to accomplish plans, or to realize intentions; a requirement for organization that is to some extent hierachical; and a reliance on the skills of gathering, interpreting, and applying information. In this conception both power and freedom are strongly rational, instrumental, and teachable. Both are construed as means toward chosen ends, rather than as ends in themselves.

Impulsive and Conditional Freedom

Rousseau is wildly contradictory on the idea of freedom. He praises unconditioned instinct as the most reliable guide for education, but at the same time he secretly and constantly manages the contingencies of Émile's environment in order to shape his pupil's experiences and ensure their proper outcome. His contradictory initiatives leave us wondering why we ought to obey instinct or impulse if we wish to be free. Rousseau says, "Let us lay it down as an incontrovertible rule that the first impulses of nature are always right."[1] But there remains the question, vividly raised by C. S. Lewis:

> Why ought we to obey instinct? Is there another instinct of a higher order directing us to do so, and a third for a still higher order directing us to obey *it?*—An infinite regress of instincts? This is presumably impossible, but nothing else will serve. From the statement about the psychological fact 'I have an impulse to do so and so' we cannot by any ingenuity derive the practical principle 'I ought to obey this impulse'.... Telling us to obey instinct is like telling us to obey 'people'. People say different things; so do instincts.[2]

John Dewey anticipated this criticism of freedom as the "free expression of impulses" when he said:

> Instincts and impulses, however they may be defined, are part of the "natural" constitution of man; a statement in which "natural" signifies "native," original. The theory assigns a certain intrinsic

rightness in this original structure, rightness in the sense of con-
ferring upon impulses a title to pass into direct action, except
when they directly and evidently interfere with similar self-
manifestation in others. The idea thus overlooks the part played
by interaction with the surrounding medium, especially the social, generating impulses and desires. These are supposed to in-
here in the "nature" of the individual when that is taken in a
primal state, uninfluenced by interaction with an environment.
The latter is thus thought of as purely external to an individual,
and as irrelevant to freedom except when it interferes with the
operation of native instincts and impulses.[3]

The real fallacy in this classic liberal view, Dewey goes on to
say, lies in the notion that

individuals have such a native or original endowment of rights,
powers, and wants that all that is required on the side of institutions and laws is to eliminate the obstructions they offer to the
"free" play of the natural equipment of individuals.[4]

Dewey's own view was that freedom depended on the regulation of antecedents and consequences vis-à-vis a particular end.
Freedom for him is a function of percipient change, that is,
change that comes about as a product of keen perception, a
sense of self, and a sense of the future. Impulse and immediacy
are, in this view, overshadowed by mediation and planning.

Paul Weiss alludes to these issues in drawing his distinction
between "native" and "conditional" freedom.[5] Every animal
has some ability by virtue of its being a particular individual,
but such ability is enjoyed at the expense of other capacities.
My particular bones and muscles make it relatively easy to
play tennis but very difficult to play the piano. The supremely
graceful swimming of a sea otter is made possible by a combination of features which makes it awkward in a tree. There is
an unavoidable interplay between freedom as ability and limitation as the consequence of that ability. The desk-bound
writer can use a quill to make words, but the nonliterate bird
can fly.

Conditional freedom is necessary for the exercise of native

freedom. I need a court, racquet, balls, partner, and good weather to play tennis. The otter needs the sea, the writer needs paper and pen, the bird a sky.

As an educational prescription, the authoritarian view that freedom must be legislated out of existence is no more helpful than Rousseau's belief that impulse is the purest expression of freedom. Dewey and Weiss, with their emphasis on the interplay between abilities and limitations, have suggested a more promising point of view from which to consider the place of freedom in education.

Disputes Over Freedom

There are in general two types of disputes over freedom. The first is disagreement on the question of who should have the right to act freely and of how extensive this right should be. The general predisposition is to believe that personal freedom is deserved and should be extensive, but as to the liberty of others we are not so sure. We are of two minds on this question because the delegation of the right to act freely is predicated on some degree of trust that the right will not be abused, and such trust usually means that the person is expected to accept the responsibility implied by the right. It is clear that while many people demand the right fewer accept the accompanying responsibility—a situation that raises suspicion as to which others can be trusted with freedom. The greater the (cultural) distance between ourselves and the "others," the greater the suspicion. This situation is a reflection of the fact that the basic terms of freedom, from which all formulations of freedom follow, are "me," "you," and "us."

This general point has provoked a great deal of controversy, much of it conducted in the name of "the people." For example, speaking for Marx and Paulo Freire, Joel Spring writes:

> Critical consciousness ... is ... a force countering the bureaucracy, which threatens to deaden the revolutionary vision and dominate the people in the very name of their freedom.[6]

"The people" does not mean, as it once did, "a people," as in "a nation," or even as in "We, the people." It now signifies ordinary people, often of a minority group, mostly poor and without significant property attachments, who are being fooled more than some of the time either by the state or by a few extraordinary people of extraordinary wealth. Appeals to the will of "the people" as moral justification for radical proposals are made almost reflexively, with bare regard for the fact that the majority of a people may not qualify as "the people," at least as the term is used here. Since the late 1970s a strong majority of "the people" in this country has suggested that schools need to have more discipline and be less libertarian even than they are now.[7] Nevertheless, Spring puts forward his libertarian view of freedom and of education as if it were "the people's" view of the proper way to consider freedom in relation to responsibility, and reason. Aside from the question of who speaks for "the people," there is a question of logic within the libertarian view of freedom that needs clarification.

A libertarian, as we have come to use the term, and as Spring uses it, means one who holds to the doctrine of a free will (in the nonmetaphysical sense of social and political independence), and to the primacy of individual liberty in thought and action. The libertarian view means, in short, taking responsibility for oneself and, to a large extent, for one's social circumstances. It should be noted first that "being free" and "being responsible" are not synonymous. One can be free in the sense that one can and does make choices, while refusing to acknowledge that responsibility is an antecedent or a consequence of choosing. Further, "being responsible" and "taking responsibility" are not identical concepts (a parent could *be* responsible for a child while acting negligently in refusing to take responsibility). In order to *take* responsibility, as the libertarian would have the people do, one must not only possess the requisite freedom to choose, one must also possess reason. Taking responsibility for one's actions and circumstances is very much what we mean when we say that a person's actions are reasoned, reasonable, rational. A "choice" without reason is what we usually call an impulse or an instinct, behavior that we all try to control, in varying degrees, by reason. One certainly cannot choose to take responsibility without recognizing a debt to reason. In taking responsibility, then, one binds oneself to the constraints of reason, and to the ethical imperative carried with them: in matters of cognition one treats evidence with justice, equal reasons are given equal consideration; in matters of ethics, action is taken as a matter of principle and not as a matter of caprice, or self-interest alone. In short, then, rationality demands consistency. Once committed to responsibility through choice, one accepts the obligation to remain so committed even when cases seem to "go against" one.

This internalization of the authority of consistent rationality is precisely what makes it possible to take responsibility, and far from being the enemy of libertarian freedom, such internalization is the necessary foundation of freedom in community/individual relations. Neither this reasoning nor this conclusion is evident in Spring's position, which emphasizes that government-controlled education produces citizens who will uphold the authority of government even in those instances when such authority may run counter to personal interest, and therefore government-controlled education must be contrary to freedom.

The second type of dispute over freedom is best understood as disagreement on the question of how freedom is to be related to other social benefits. Freedom is associated, in one form or another, with a range of social benefits such as security, status, dignity, and equality. Often these benefits are assumed to be the results of freedom, but sometimes they are treated as preconditions. Most social liabilities are identified with the lack of freedom.

It is important to realize that a desire for one or more of these social benefits is not necessarily a desire for freedom. They are not the same sorts of desire, and they may be contradictory in some instances. For example, one person's sense of security and status may be achieved best in a steady bond of common dependence and sacrifice with a number of other individuals, a relationship in which the right to act freely is much less important than the stability and reliability of the bond. A person in such circumstances may experience a freedom of mind or a feeling of freedom because of an achieved satisfaction in a relation that is objectively unfree. Freedom as a subjective state of mind is not to be confused with freedom as a set of objective conditions in the relations among individuals.

The determination of the place of freedom as one social value among other social values and benefits is difficult and sometimes impossible to resolve. In democratic theory freedom must meet the requirement of not trespassing on the grounds of equality. Tocqueville and J. S. Mill asked what would become of freedom in a society in which conditions became more and more equal, and they concluded that freedom as a social value would be subordinated to the value of equality, and that eventually this subordinate relation would produce a tyranny of the majority in substitution for individual freedom. Neither was pleased by this probability.

We see then, that freedom always needs to be defined and evaluated in relation to other social values and the social benefits we desire to share, and in relation to reasoning. It is conceptually very difficult to deal with freedom as a subjective state of mind or an independent value because it is basically a term of relation. In this regard freedom is similar to power as they are both essentially relational concepts.

My interest now is in developing a reconceptualized logic of freedom that takes account of these principles, and that demonstrates the close connection between freedom and the social value of education.

The Logic of Freedom

In this section I propose an argument and a model for the "best use" of the concept of freedom in the elucidation of educational theory and practice. Both the argument and the model owe their beginnings to Joel Feinberg's essay "The Idea of a Free Man."[8]

Since Mill's classic statement that the absence of coercion is the sufficient and necessary condition for freedom, the individualist/liberal view has been enlarged to include two amendments: (1) other than human coercion, there must be an absence of natural conditions that prevent the chosen activity, and (2) one must have the executive power to do that which one wishes. This enlarged liberal view then became a two-sided concept of freedom: freedom from . . . and freedom to . . . . Along with Feinberg, I would argue that although there is a conceptual difference between "free from" and "free to," separating them does not lead anywhere because all cases of freedom have them *both* as attributes; they are head and tail of a single coin. Feinberg offers a single concept to replace, and simplify, the double-concept analysis. He does this by defining "constraint" as anything that prevents one from doing something, and then proposing that all constraints can be considered along two dimensions: the positive/negative dimension and the internal/external dimension. Combining these dimensions yields four categories of constraint: (1) *Internal Positive,* such as headaches, obsessive thoughts, compulsive desires; (2) *Internal Negative,* such as ignorance, weakness, deficiencies in talent or skill; (3) *External Positive,* such as barred windows, locked doors, and pointed bayonets; and (4) *External Negative,* such as poverty, lack of transportation, and the like. The following diagram helps to clarify the relations among these categories of constraint:

Categories of constraint

	Positive	*Negative*
Internal	obsession	ignorance
External	guns, locks	poverty

In each instance there is a "free from" and a "free to" aspect to the constraint in question, but neither of these is as important as determining the type of constraint most relevant to a particular problem of freedom.

Autonomy is another idea central to this analysis of freedom, and its importance can be demonstrated through a contrast with anomie. Autonomous means self-governing, or self-regulating, and it implies an ordered structure of wants, purposes, and ideals. The order makes it possible to decide between conflicting alternatives on a basis of hierarchical relations.

Anomie, according to Durkheim, is a defective condition in persons who have had no success at ordering their personal ideals, desires, intentions, and commitments into some sort of hierarchy. The lack of such order leaves the person vulnerable to internal action jams and motivation jumbles. Free to do anything, one has difficulty deciding what to do. This condition is a sort of inhibiting disorientation, an internal constraint, that stands in the way of accomplishing objectives. Such absence of order, rules, and hierarchical structure is what people often call freedom; the existentialist might call it dreadful freedom. From outside, though, it looks very much as if the person thus free is not free to act in ways that he or she might wish. Instead of conduct regulated and assisted by a system of stop and go, yield and "caution when wet," one is bashed and bandied about by the pulse of impulse and the force of habit in the fashion of the amusement park ride called "Bumper Cars." Anomie leads to a view of freedom as episodic entertainment, and a culture of contradictory self-interests, of perpetual variation unguided by any sense of purpose or community.

Autonomy, though, does not mean "being free to do anything." It means self-governing. "Autonomic" has the sense of self-regulation within the context of a larger whole. The autonomic nervous system, for example, is concerned mainly with regulating the smooth muscles and glands, but it is not subject to strict voluntary control; nevertheless it is dependent on the brain and spinal cord. It is a system, with organization and uniformity; it is self-regulating but not free of the larger whole that sustains it. In the same way, one can speak of a person's behavior as being probabalistically determined by the (social and physical) system that sustains him, but not wholly determined if at any time a mental state can influence the function and effect of that system, say, by acting morally without reward. One thinks of the possibility of altruism as an influence on a social system of rewards. Such a mental state, which serves to regulate behavior in the absence of external conditioners, may be called autonomy.

Autonomy, as used in this analysis, signifies that a person's wants and purposes are related to each other in a hierarchy ordered on the basis of held values and commitments, that the person is internally organized, has reasons, and chooses accordingly. This sense of freedom is very different from that of anomie, a condition in which one has no means for assessing why one does something. It would appear that organization may be as necessary to the concept of freedom as it is to power.

For me, neither freedom nor power is conceivable in the absence of organization, and the traditional antipathy or dichotomy between autonomy and hierarchy seems fundamentally mistaken. Autonomy is an achievement that requires hierarchy, both internally in the organization of wants and commitments, and externally in the organization of social relations through laws and customs. The idea of autonomy (*auto:* self + *nomos:* law) itself contains the principle of governing, which is the systematic application of rules that define the structure of social relations and preserve a given community's claims to the security and regularity that, it is hoped, protect justice from the devastation of competitive self-interests.

The essence of freedom is to be found in the configurations of constraint which are at the same time the most salient characteristics of organization. As Freud so convincingly argued in *Civilization and Its Discontents,* it is the governance of instinct gratification by means of cooperative configurations of constraint which provides the basis of civilization itself, which is security. Civilization is the transformation of anomie into autonomy through organizational hierarchy.

The important theoretical point is that the concept of freedom is related to power through organization, and that both are properly understood as partly psychological, partly social, and always instrumental. The psychological aspect of freedom is found in the internal organization of wants, purposes, and ideals—intentions—which tends toward hierarchy in a self-governing individual. The sociological aspect is found in the fact that freedom is a relational term, whose basic components are "me" and "you" and "us." The social character of the concept is also manifest in the necessity of taking responsibility for the consequences of one's acting freely. Responsibility is one of the essential terms in the vocabulary of social life. Being "free from" is never total; it is always a matter of more or less, and it stands always in relation with being "free to." The two are found together in every question of freedom, and they are defined in context, not in the abstract. Freedom is a term of contextual relations among people, and as such it is always partly social.

The instrumental aspect of freedom can be identified by asking the question "What for?" when a claim for freedom is made. People claim freedoms for reasons of their usefulness or necessity in doing, being, or becoming something. Freedom is a term that describes the circumstantial mediation of intention. We do not often speak of "wanting to be free to be free." Rather, we speak of being free to work, love, express ourselves, and move about as we like, or being free from unjust and unwanted constraints on favored activities. There is always something that freedom leads away from or toward, a change of conditions that is valued above the status quo, that freedom is used to achieve. Freedom per se, considered independently of its instrumental value, is a categorical error of the imagination. Freedoms are not ends, they are means to other ends.

One freedom comes at the expense of another, just as one

capacity is enjoyed at the expense of another. The consequence of one freedom or one capacity is the limitation of another. Freedoms themselves are constraints on other (possible) freedoms, while all freedoms are made possible by constraints of one kind or another. It is a fact of human life that not all freedoms can ever be enjoyed at the same time, and it is another fact that no human being can exist outside of a limiting configuration of constraints. The key to understanding problems of freedom lies in understanding these configurations of constraints.

My argument for a best use of freedom, keeping in mind its structurally ambiguous and essentially contestable character, has led so far to a description with three emphases. Perhaps a summary would help to clarify these. Freedom is a concept I use to indicate the status of constraints that are relative to a plan for action. As such, freedom's psychological basis is rational because: (1) it involves making percipient judgments about actual and anticipated conditions, and (2) it is autonomous, or self-governing, and thus requires an internal hierarchical ordering of wants, purposes, and commitments. Freedom's sociological basis is relational because: (3) it always occurs as an interplay between capacities and the limitations that are the necessary consequences of those capacities, (4) capacities are always subject to conditional circumstances in the environment, (5) freedom is of value only in some connection with other social benefits, and (6) the basic terms of a freedom relationship ("me," "you," and "us") are inherently social themselves. Its instrumental basis lies in (7) the diagnosis of those constraints that keep a person from implementing a plan for action.

Freedom, then, is a concept with rational, relational, and diagnostic qualities that are joined together in the process of choosing and judging plans for action in a context of constraints. In one sense, freedom describes one's satisfaction with, or the acceptability of, a particular configuration of constraints relative to a particular plan for action. Unfreedom describes dissatisfaction and unacceptability with regard to constraints.

The method implied by this line of reasoning for solving problems of freedom is primarily a method of diagnosis. A problem of freedom must be restated and reconceived as a problem of particular constraints. Once this has been accomplished, the problem itself will have been transformed into a simpler, more manageable form through a process designed to identify and isolate the most salient aspects of a complex configuration of constraints and to indicate the most promising actions to take. This method of diagnosis is related to the fiction and finance forms of power through its emphasis on the control of information. Such control includes the ability to gather, interpret, and apply information that is relevant to a particular constraint, or pattern of constraints, which stands in the way of realizing an intention. In this way, one can argue that exercising power and acting freely are similar in their reliance on the rational abilities needed to identify and overcome constraints on a plan for action.

The Constraint Matrix

A problem of freedom arises when an intention is blocked or frustrated by constraints. Constraints often occur in bunches and often they are difficult to sort out. Unsorted, they may appear overwhelming because we mistakenly identify possible (suspected) constraints as actual constraints and thus compound the factors that we imagine to be blocking our plan for action. Once identified and sorted out, the configuration of actual constraints will at least look different and likely be more manageable. The important first step toward the solution of a problem of freedom is diagnosing the configuration of constraints relevant to the particular situation.

The constraint matrix on page 133 is a conceptual instrument to be used for identifying and sorting out the critical constraints and their relationships to each other in a particular problem context. By using the matrix one can translate problems of freedom into forms that are accessible to practical solutions, and can expose the values that are being sought and served by the appeals made on freedom as a means.

The Constraint Matrix

Categories of constraint

	Psychobiological		Societal	Equivocal
	1st person	3d person	Societal	Equivocal
Active				
Abeyant				

Modes

Definition of terms: *Active:* effective by virtue of its presence; *Abeyant:* effective by virtue of its absence; *Psychobiological:* capable of both psychic and physiological activity; an integration of these; *Societal:* pertaining to organized society; legal, economic, and geographical conditions, institutions both formal and informal; other material and interpersonal relations; *Equivocal:* of doubtful location; indeterminate, enigmatic; having two or more significations.

I think of the matrix as a template that can be used to reconceive any problematic situation in which an intention, or plan for action, is frustrated by some constraint(s). This image was inspired by George Kelly's phenomenological theory of behavior in which he used a similar idea to help explain the development of an individual's cognitive categories used to exercise control over events that affect one's life.[9]

It is important to remember that the matrix is no more than a contraption with formal properties and fixed categories. It does not provide any of the contextual information necessary for determining the exact sort of relationships among discrete constraints that inhibit freedoms. It only provides a method for specifying these relationships once the constraints have been sorted out. To extend Matthew Arnold's metaphor, I might say that the matrix is a machine used in the production of freedoms.

Modes and Categories of the Matrix

Constraints can work in two ways: either something that one needs is not present, not in one's possession; or something that is present interferes with one's intention. The latter I call the active mode (effective by virtue of its presence), and the former I call abeyant (effective by virtue of its absence). Abeyant also carries the sense of latency which is important, especially in the psychobiological category. For example, a child who wishes to learn but has difficulty concentrating may be suffering from a nutritional deficiency—the absence of sufficient protein and carbohydrate to maintain an adequate blood-sugar level. This is not a permanent condition, and hypothetically the child's blood sugar has a latent adequacy that can be attained through a change in diet. Nevertheless, for a time (before it is diagnosed) the child suffers a limitation on the freedom to learn that can be called an abeyant psychobiological constraint.

A child with a similar problem in concentrating may, on the other hand, have a headache, or may manifest a chemically induced form of "hyperactivity." These constraints are effective because the pain, or the culprit chemicals are present, and therefore active. Such constraints as these require quite different remedies than do abeyant ones.

The three categories—psychobiological, societal, and equivocal—are useful for locating the placement of a given constraint. It is not always clear whether an actual constraint emanates from oneself, from another individual whose position is important to one's plan for action, from an identifiable but nonspecific "social force," or from a non-identifiable source whose effects are objects of strong belief. For example, a member of a minority group may lose a chance to be hired in a government agency and the formal reason given might be "not qualified," with no further explanation. Certainly a plan has been frustrated, and a problem of freedom arises in the applicant's mind. There would be a tendency to blame "prejudice" as the actual constraint, but this identification does not do much to solve the problem. Where can this "prejudice" be found? Some possible answers are: (1) in the mind and behavior of the applicant who may be hostile and suspicious to the point of paranoia when confronted with certain pressured situations, and whose traits make the employer doubt that the applicant could get along with other employees (1st person psychobiological/active); (2) in the mind of the interviewer who never had any sincere intention to hire the applicant no matter how qualified, but whose views are contrary to the public policy and general disposition of the agency as a whole (3d person psychobiological/active); (3) in the quota system for hiring required by law which temporarily excluded all applicants in our subject's category (societal/active); (4) in "the bureaucracy" that failed to process the application through negligence, no single responsible cause for which can be isolated (equivocal/abeyant).

Any of these is a plausible explanation for the source of the actual constraint. Of course, more than one explanation may be required for a complete understanding. The point is that by using the matrix to explore possibilities systematically, one can generate a set of alternative hypotheses, test them, and arrive at a revised formulation of the problem which may lead to a more satisfactory judgment about what new plan for action is required for solving the problem of freedom.

In giving examples for each of the matrix categories and discussing some of the techniques for applying this simple machine to the production of freedom, I must stress that a real context is required for any concrete analysis, and that my examples are only hypothetical. Nevertheless, one can follow the principles in theory and then provide one's own real examples of freedom problems once the principles have become familiar.

Psychobiological

In this category constraints are understood to be situated in single individuals. A distinction needs to be made between the person whose problem of freedom is being scrutinized and other significant people whose influence is constraining but who should not be thought of as representing a more general social phenomenon.[10] In the active mode, as already illustrated, prejudice can work as a constraint on a personal level in an otherwise unprejudicial situation. In the abeyant mode, ignorance or a skill deficiency could be identified as an actual constraint either in the person whose plan is frustrated (e.g., the student who wants to get a job as a journalist but who cannot learn to write grammatically or spell correctly), or the constraint may lie in a person who is the (partial) cause of the frustration (e.g., the student's English teacher who was unresponsive, did not require a sufficiently high standard of grammatical skill, or provide enough instruction and directed practice to ensure that the skills would be learned). Determining whether the student is constitutionally incapable of learning the required skills because of an irremediable biological problem (arrested mental development due to early and severe malnutrition or hypothyroidism), or whether the problem is remediable (perhaps there is a lack of motivation due to low self-regard, or maybe the teacher in question is incompetent and could be replaced) makes all the difference in assaying the range of possible solutions to the problem. One needs to know whether one is confronting a phobia, stubbornness, ignorance, a fetish, misanthropy, prejudice, malnutrition, physical weakness, a tumor, drug side-effects, or incompetence, before one can even state fully what the problem is.

Societal

Sometimes a plan for action is frustrated not through any fault of one's own or through the effects of another individual, but through certain social conditions. In the active mode, society is regulated by habits, customs, and mores that have passed into the consciousness of its members as firm expectations, as codes and rules for conduct. In addition to these there are common, statutory, and constitutional laws that constrain some freedoms while protecting others. The history of *Brown* v. *Board of Education of Topeka*,[11] which made "separate but equal" schools illegal for black and white students, is strong evidence that local customs can constrain the implementation of constitutional laws and may require officials to take actions contrary to the law, all in the name of someone's freedom to carry out a plan for action. Quota systems in education and employment are constraints of an active social kind, as are court-ordered school busing and compulsory attendance laws; the information-gathering and record-keeping of public schools, the FBI, and credit agencies; the certification requirements for certain professionals; traffic laws, building codes, and zoning regulations; taxes, elections, armies, and "nuclear deterrence."

Contrasting with these active constraints are some abeyant ones such as poverty (lack of money), geographical limitation or isolation (lack of transportation), "rootlessness" (lack of community or family place), and various other forms of disorganization (lack of cohesion and structure among people who might have a common grievance, a mutual problem, or similar needs that cannot be satisfied individually). Coming up against a locked door (active societal constraint) is not the same as coming up against an empty purse or a group of fellow tenants who cannot be organized to confront a negligent landlord (abeyant societal constraint) when there are rats in the building. One can see the rats themselves, or the landlord, prejudice, greed, capitalism, the laws, poverty, garbage, "urban rot," or the lack of community organization as the actual constraint(s). How one sees these possibilities, and the configuration of constraints which emerges from the analysis will determine the most promising approach to take in resolving the problem.

Equivocal

This is the most difficult category of constraint and the most fascinating. Constraints of this type may exist in fact or merely in the imagination, but they are always very effective and elude analytic reduction. It is not surprising that some of these constraints share the structural ambiguity and essential contestability of freedom itself.

Sophocles expressed dramatically the strong active constraint that "fate" exerted on Antigone in her course of action against Creon and the new order that he represented.

> Antigone (to Creon): Nor did I think your orders were so strong that you, a mortal man, could over-run the gods' unwritten and unfailing laws. Not now, nor yesterday's, they always live, and no one knows their origin in time. So not through fear of any man's proud spirit would I be likely to neglect these laws, and draw on myself the gods' sure punishment. I knew that I must die; how could I not?[12]

Kafka has portrayed better than anyone else the terrible, unidentifiable, and equivocal "them":

> "There can be no doubt—" said K., quite softly, for he was elated by the breathless attention of the meeting; in that stillness a subdued hum was audible which was more exciting than the wildest applause—"there can be no doubt that behind all the actions of this court of justice, that is to say in my case, behind my arrest and today's interrogation, there is a great organization at work. An organization which not only employs corrupt warders, oafish Inspectors, and Examining Magistrates of whom the best that can be said is that they recognize their own limitations, but also has at its disposal a judicial hierarchy of high, indeed of the highest rank, with an indispensable and numerous retinue of servants, clerks, police, and other assistants, perhaps even hangmen, I do not shrink from that word. And the significance of this great organization, gentlemen? It consists in this, that innocent persons are accused of guilt, and senseless proceedings are put in motion against them, mostly without effect, it is true, as in my own case."[13]

If "they" won't allow it, it can't be done, but if "they" wish it, it shall be.

There is an old and extensive literature about "nature," or "creation," which suggests the certain futility of opposing it when the path to true freedom is in fact through an acceptance of nature's own patterns. For Lao Tzu, the way (the Tao) is:

> a source of life, the various stages in the formation of the universe are stages in the development of life, and from the central principle a current of life spreads by degrees throughout "creation."

> The real, one and multiple, is no other than a life principle, which is sometimes concentrated in a single point and sometimes dispersed among the infinite varieties of beings, where it divides into a variety of particular life functions.[14]

The great American voice in this literature is Thoreau, whose philosophical advice in *Walden* was to find freedom in sitting on a pumpkin: "I would rather sit on a pumpkin and have it all to myself than be crowded on a velvet cushion."[15]

Of course the source of all these ideas is "God," whose equivocal meaning has had the planet's speculators guessing for as long as anyone has guessed about anything. It is still the case that fate, nature, the Tao, God, and even "cosmic energy" have tremendous constraining effects on the believers' individual freedoms. Determinism, instinct, absolute yielding, divine commandments, the life force, or the more mundane bureaucratic controls "they" exercise deep in the shadows of secrecy—these are all active constraints even though they are nowhere (everywhere?) to be found. A special type of equivocal constraint, one that concerns all of us, is "red tape."

Red Tape. By complaining about red tape, people usually mean that some agency takes too long to act, that there are too many constraints on themselves and on the agency, and that many if not all of these constraints are unnecessary. It is sometimes the case that such complaining comes about before any actual experience with the agency in question. It may come about as a form of "hasty generalization" made on the basis of previous experience with other agencies, or it may come about as a result of listening to stories of others who suffered long delays in some bureaucratic entanglements. In any case, the important point is that our assumption that red tape is a remote, inevitable, and almost overwhelming constraint often becomes a constraint in itself. Such a surmise is sufficient in many cases to prevent one from even trying to penetrate an agency's organization and regulations.

However, if regulations are understood to be reasonable, and if their number in a specific case is seen as at least manageable, then they are likely to be perceived less as red tape and more as necessary or purposeful constraints that cause annoying but justifiable delay. Achieving this understanding depends on at least two conditions: (1) the skills of analysis necessary for any sort of diagnosis and general comprehension of constraints, and (2) an appreciation for the source and purpose of red tape, an appreciation that makes it possible to discriminate between the paralysis that comes of thinking of the evils of red tape per se, and the possibilities that come from thinking of particular problems caused by red tape. The view that *all* red tape is pointless and excessive, leaving one helpless and frustrated, is a view that itself constitutes a psychological constraint, but one that is remediable. The remediation begins with the realization that we all contribute to the necessity for and the existence of red tape by insisting that our public agencies, the government at large, be representative and display compassion for individuals.[16]

Herbert Kaufman neatly summarizes the connections between the proliferation of red tape and the very nature of our society:

> Were we a less differentiated society, the blizzard of official paper might be less severe and the labyrinths of official processes less tortuous. Had we more trust in one another and in our public

officers and employees, we would not feel impelled to limit discretion by means of lengthy, minutely detailed directives and prescriptions or to subject public and private actions to check after check. If our polity were less democratic, imperfect though our democracy may be, the government would not respond as readily to the innumerable claims on it for protection and assistance. Diversity, distrust, and democracy thus cause the profusion of constraints and the unwieldiness of the procedures that afflict us. It is in this sense that we bring it on ourselves.[17]

If Kaufman is correct, and I think he is, we must not fill the air with angry proposals to get rid of red tape by reducing the size of government, or by either centralizing or decentralizing authority, or by replacing government control with privately initiated service or management enterprises. We must instead learn to deal with the labyrinths and to teach others how to deal with them, too. After all, we made the labyrinths and it is our responsibility to make them navigable.[18]

That the constraints of red tape can be overcome has been demonstrated by the well-educated and by the wealthy who can buy the effects of education. Skills in constraint diagnosis can help us to deal with the constraints of red tape, and as we do so the constraints themselves will become less oppressive. These skills are both learnable and teachable, and those agencies whose red tape is a public problem must themselves shoulder some of the responsibility for bringing such skills to the public. The field offices of the IRS and the Veterans Administration, and the thirty or more Federal Information Centers in urban areas around the country are examples of how this education effort can be planned with considerable effect. However, it would seem that the primary responsibility for such public education rests with the institutions already set up for the purpose of public education—schools, colleges, and universities. This responsibility will become an educational priority of the special and urgent significance it deserves only if educators in policymaking positions can be convinced that its neglect constitutes in effect an unjustified limitation on an individual's capacity for full participation in the social and legal rights of the nation.

The Absurd. The last remaining category of constraint is a ghostly abstraction: equivocal and abeyant. Is it not absurd even to think about a constraint on a person's freedoms which is of doubtful existence, is unplaceable in any case, and has its effect by virtue of being absent? Well, the best answers are yes and no.

To describe this category, I need to borrow from a philosophical literature that is best known by the rather imprecise name of existentialism, and that includes the work of such diverse thinkers as Dostoyevsky, Kierkegaard, Kafka, Husserl, Heidegger, Jaspers, Marcel, Nietzsche, Sartre, de Beauvoir, and Camus. The two most prominent themes developed in this literature, alienation and the absurd, share an emphasis on "separation," but each gives the word a somewhat different meaning. Alienation refers to the social separation between individuals and between one individual's "Being" and "mere existence," whereas the absurd suggests the psychological and intellectual separation between a desire for complete explanation and the essential impossibility of ever getting one. Camus speaks of the absurd this way:

> I realize that if through science I can seize phenomena and enumerate them, I cannot, for all that, apprehend the world. Were I to trace its entire relief with my finger, I should not know any more. And you give me the choice between a description that is sure but that teaches me nothing and hypotheses that claim to teach me but that are not sure.[19]

The terrible paradox that Camus perceives is that man has lucidity, yet simultaneously is surrounded by opaque walls; we are lucid enough to perceive the walls but unable to see a way out or even to guess why the walls are there.

The absurd comes to stand for the fact that the world will

never be coherent to the human mind, and yet that mind will never stop wishing for—and working for—a coherence that will help to make sense of ethical and logical rules. The world is indifferent to reason, to all of human existence.

For Camus, the sole significant datum is the absurd, but it is not the world itself that constitutes the absurd. The absurd depends as much upon man as upon the world. To understand the world one must apprehend all of its events in all of their relations. This is impossible for, as Dewey suggests, the limits of man's knowledge due to the effects of context are finite, though indefinite. Nonetheless, as Camus vividly illustrates, there is in man a nostalgia, a wild longing for clarity, a need for familiarity, an appetite for certainty. "The absurd is essentially a divorce (between the man considering the world and the world considered). It lies in neither of the elements compared; it is born of their confrontation."[20] As such, the absurd is an event; it is a process, and it carries the same implications of qualitative relation to context as were mentioned above.

The absurd, for Camus, is not merely the consequence of this confrontation; it takes on the significance of a hostile force, and thus becomes a *source* of confrontation in its own right. One has to deal with "it" actively, for "it" becomes active in the consciousness once one is aware of it.

Camus himself is careful to say that he has not defined the absurd. Rather, he has given "an enumeration of the feelings that may admit of the absurd." Like Dewey's "background" and "selective interest," Camus' concept of the absurd is an understood quality that is not available for complete articulate definition, but is nonetheless effective by its very presence. He approaches it from many angles:

> At the heart of all beauty lies something inhuman, and these hills, the softness of the sky, the outline of these trees at this very minute lose the illusory meaning with which we had clothed them, henceforth more remote than a lost paradise.... that denseness and that strangeness of the world is the absurd.[21]

I merely want to remain in this middle path where the intelligence can remain clear. If that is its pride, I see no sufficient reason for giving it up. . . . Perhaps this notion will become clearer if I risk this shocking statement: the absurd is sin without God.[22]

The absurd is lucid reason noting its limits. Belief in the absurd as a fundamental condition of human life (I doubt that any other species is plagued in this fanciful and fantastic way) constrains one's ability to believe in anything more stable and concrete than oneself, or longer lived than any individual.

Summary

This model of freedom's logic is marked off from others by a set of three characteristics:

1. It requires that issues of social importance which appeal to freedom in some sense be treated not as if "freedom" were well understood, but just the reverse. At the start of the analysis, it is assumed that "freedom" has not been defined and is *not* well understood. The point is not to define it directly.

2. The model requires that at least one participant in the discussion be capable of irony, that is, capable of seeing complexity from a distance without self-righteousness and capable of imagining the experience of others to the degree that the other's sense of freedom can be read as a matrix of constraints.

3. The model and the necessary skills can be taught: therefore, freedom (as a process of diagnosing constraints) can be taught. Insofar as knowing precisely what constraints *are* renders one more likely to become free in a given set of circumstances, then freedom can be taught. Insofar as diagnosing constraints is relevant to solving practical problems of contextual freedoms, the model is a practical, if partial, answer to the problem of freedom in education.

The following are the important assumptions of the model that have been either discussed or implied:

1. Freedom is never actually valued for itself alone; it is always a means to other values, other ends.

2. Disputes over freedom are best understood as attempts to link freedom with other social benefits—these social benefits are treated as results of, or contributions to freedom, and liabilities are connected with the absence of freedom. Thus freedom is identified with a whole range of social benefits, and there is great difficulty in ascertaining the status of freedom among them.

3. Freedom is a word that stands for active relationships, and as such it cannot be defined in isolation but must be taken contextually.

4. The active relationships that identify freedom are triadic: P is (is not) free from 0 to do (not do, become, not become) X.

5. Human behavior is a product of many variables, such as the historical and physical environment, the psychological environment, social and economic status, genetic and dispositional traits, knowledge, imagination, and experience, to name a few. With respect to influencing a gain in a certain freedom relationship, one has to determine which of the many possible influences are the actual, operating ones. And it is just here that the constraint matrix is of considerable use.

6. One cannot reasonably value any particular freedom situation without approving of the associated unfreedom relationships. It is morally impossible to approve all freedoms.

7. The effective operation of choosing is what freedom means on a personal level; there are skills involved in choosing and these can be taught.

8. If freedom lies in the cognitive skills of scrutinizing vague preferences until the preferences constitute performable choices, then freedom of thought is central to all other freedoms. Insofar as education means developing skills of free thought, education becomes crucial to freedoms of all kinds.

9. Choosing should be construed as the formation of preferences out of a conflict of constraints and possibilities.

The activity of freedom, in my view, is not pure cognition. It is a sort of practical mastery made possible by increments in knowledge, and the application in practice of this knowledge. It is, in short, a technique for dealing with something that obstructs our doing what we want to do. Learning this technique will help protect us from the charge that we are not doing well what we should do well, when we could do better. We need to prepare ourselves and others for the situations that demand choices, especially ethical choices.

The mastery of technique does not assure the fulfillment of responsibilities, but that technique does help us to meet those responsibilities if and when we attempt to do so. We will blunder, no matter what. But we can also try to reduce our blunders to a minimum through some sort of controlled anticipation, and by developing skills in choosing and judging.

I am mindful that in our models and programs for freedom we must monitor a tendency to make others look and think just as we do ourselves. What we choose to emphasize in discussing freedom will reflect the particular values that we assume are necessary to support our claims about the meaning of freedom. And this reminds me—again—that freedom is a mediation between values and persons; it is not a value in itself.

Like Dewey, "I shall begin to believe that we care more for freedom than we do for imposing our own beliefs upon others in order to subject them to our will, when I see that the main purpose of our schools and other institutions is to develop powers of unremitting and discriminating observation and judgment."[23]

Part III /

THE ETHICS
OF EDUCATION

In this concluding chapter a case is made for the claim that education now has an ethical responsibility to focus on the rudiments of power and the skills of acting freely. The case rests on several propositions about what is basic and indispensable for getting on as decent people in a society that is so thoroughly dependent on so many organizations and institutions, and that still strongly favors a democratic system of governing.

6 /

Power and the
Skills of Freedom

One of the oldest and best questions raised in civilizations of all kinds, a question greater than any of the answers yet proposed, is what the purpose of (an) education ought to be. Civilization requires education of some kind. But what kind? What needs to be learned, by whom, and for what reasons?

I ask the question yet again, but in a slightly altered form: What ought to be taught that is basic and indispensable for getting on as decent people in our modern social milieux? My answer will be no more than a prolegomenon to a revised ethics of education. I would like to offer an alternative view of the difficulties we face in moral education, a view to be contrasted with the current well-known theories in that area.[1]

This question is difficult to think about, let alone answer, without wandering off into the heights of metaphysical abstraction where that which is least substantial tends to dominate everything else that is concrete, familiar, and real. Caught up in such speculations, one is tempted to concentrate too much on the forms of Perfection and too little on the forms of actual social relations. Thus, Plato took slavery for granted in the ethical architecture of his perfect Republic. On the other hand, there is a danger of ending up dead-weary with tedious, familiar little lists that amount to minor variations on what, out of habit, we continue to call "the basics." Or one might end up with an equally tedious but longer list of "self-culture" skills and a self-promotional guide to the talents of narcissism.

Between these two very different sorts of attraction to extreme simplicity, one for the perfect truth and one for the real self, there lies a third perspective—an affinity for the more transactional, contextual, organizational, and problematical; a focus on the world through the politics of social and personal experience. This is a world where things are always changing, skipping from precise to vague, and where plans and arrangements are never clear for long. It contains all that does good or harm. There is little that is exact in this world, and those who care most for perfection will be most uncomfortable. Each of these three perspectives is represented in the most common and notable answers given to the question being considered here, though not always without some aspects of the other two. As an introduction to the argument that I will present below, I would like to summarize in the briefest terms the main answers that have been given to the problem of defining education's purpose. The range of answers is not wide, but there are several distinct and representative points of view that deserve notice.

Five Views on the Purpose of (an) Education

The first answer (but "first" here has no chronological significance, as all of these answers have been offered at many different times) is related to the idea of delight, and to the hedonic principle that holds pleasurable states of mind to be intrinsically more desirable than anything else. The purpose of education in this view is exposure to that which gives delight, and to that which enriches one's well-being. Whitehead summarized this view with the phrase "exposure to greatness," whereas Matthew Arnold spoke of "getting to know, on all the matters which most concern us, the best which has been thought and said in the world." In this way of thinking it is sometimes assumed that "the great" and "the best" will produce the most pleasure—or at least the most pleasurable state of mind for those students so engaged. In learning what gives delight, one learns to delight in learning, and eventually, as Aristotle suggested, the greatest happiness will come in contemplation.

The second notion of education's purpose pertains more to high social policy and politics. Education is necessary to ensure, at the highest level of confidence, that those who have the power and the responsibility to make decisions which affect the social welfare will be informed and motivated to make these decisions well and with good conscience. It is life with others more than life with ideas that requires education, and the purpose of education is shaped by efforts to improve the moral quality of that life.

The third answer ties education to self-preservation, insisting that it teach us how to make a living. There are two senses to "making a living." The more obvious one, of course, is the attainment of an income level sufficient to provide the wherewithal for basic needs and an acceptable standard of living. The second sense has to do with elevating existence into a life worth living, a life of social worth and personal satisfaction. To be economically safe is by no means to be psychologically or spiritually safe, and both are necessities of a life that is worth the living.

The fourth answer is partly an extension of the third; that is, it suggests that education should teach us to share in some tradition of value of which one becomes a part. In this view, education helps us to choose some values and reject others according to some pattern of preference and justification. It gives us principles that are used to help decide ethical dilemmas, and to which one can appeal in times of confusion and stress, as well as in times of ebullience. Such a conception of education stresses the importance of sharing in the historical community, which provides a deep sense of stability and continuity rarely if ever achieved by individuals alone.

The fifth answer, the most abstract and comprehensive of the lot, and perhaps the least practical, conceives education's purpose as the development of irony. In this view education is seen as the cure for innocence and all forms of parochial priggishness. It becomes the remedy for pharisaical hypocrisy, and the essential precondition for the ironic view of life, which allows for a balanced and appreciative perception of the complex in all its wondrous forms.

There may be other families of reply which one could add to my list, and certainly there are better ways of describing those I have chosen, but these five represent most of what educational philosophy has produced on the question of education's purpose. Of course, each answer often appears in some combination with the others, and only rarely in the form I have used for differentiating them here.

Given the analysis of power and the logic of freedom developed in this book, it is clear that none of these answers is a satisfactory definition of the purpose of education. To be satisfactory now, an answer to the question—"What ought to be taught that is basic and indispensable for getting on as decent persons in our modern social milieux?"—has to emphasize the importance of knowledge about power and the skills of freedom. To do less is to neglect the two most important things education can contribute to the preservation of democratic institutions—a broader distribution of power, and a greater number of people capable of self-governing behavior.

I would like to begin my answer by exploring the nature of the question.

Instinct, Bewilderment, and Education

Since civilization weakens instinct and encourages an increasingly long period of dependence for the young, education in how to get along becomes both more necessary and more leisurely as time goes on. Initiation into civilized society is carried out in a program of prolonged participation in organized social settings, the schools being chief among them since the beginning of this century. These settings help produce habits of interdependence and needs for organization that extend well beyond the family.

Education, which began as a subsidy for instinct and now substitutes for it, has long been necessary for teaching civilized individuals how to deal with "nature," but this only hints at the irony to come. Now, having come out of the woods into town, having lost the sharp sense of survival, and having learned how to accept living with machines ever present, we must learn how to deal with *people*. Education is required for learning how to deal with ourselves. This is the irony of civilization and the burden of education: we have passed from instinctual awareness to cultivated bewilderment and on to an uneasy solitude, and as a result, we must now be reeducated to an awareness of what it means to be ourselves among others. For the first time in our history other people are the major problem with which we have to deal; lots of other people in all kinds of groups.[2] What should this education include?

For one thing, such an education must include a study of human biography, which is the product of tension between the forces of impulsive expression and practical constraint, between instinct gratification and the need for social structure and security, between id and ego. As we grow, this tension becomes a battle of beliefs, and the character of this tension is taken up as a proper focus of education. Indeed this has been the theme for a great deal of psychological study of education. And as Liam Hudson has written:

> While psychologists may have had little direct experimental influence over what people do, there can be not the slightest doubt that we have contributed in a massive way to what they believe. Easily the most influential aspect of this contribution has been our promotion of an attitude to upbringing, education, and the running of society that is broadly liberated or free. This set of beliefs I shall call the permissive attitude.[3]

The promotion of this set of attitudes, through professional psychologists, is generally traced to Freud. Many people believe that his brilliant theoretical explanation of the relation between suppression and neurosis is (1) correct, and (2) grounds for concluding that suppression is wrong and bad whereas unrestrained freedom of impulsive expression is right and good. At least one of these beliefs is mistaken. Granting that Freud may have been correct, it would be useful to hear what he had to say about the application of his theory of suppression to education.

In his *New Introductory Lectures on Psychoanalysis,* published in 1933, Freud wrote:

> Let us make ourselves clear as to what the first task of education is. The child must learn to control his instincts. It is impossible to give him liberty to carry out all his impulses without restriction. To do so would be a very instructive experiment for child-psychologists; but life would be impossible for the parents and the children themselves would suffer grave damage, which would show itself partly at once and partly in later years. Accordingly, education must inhibit, forbid and suppress, and this has abundantly been seen to in all periods of history. But we have learnt from analysis that precisely this suppression of instincts involves the risk of neurotic illness. . . . Thus education has to find its way between the Scylla of non-interference and the Charybdis of frustration.[4]

Permissiveness is certainly not the right word for describing Freud's own view of education and the problem of neurotic illness. His general idea was that education should control insubordinate instincts by inhibiting, suppressing, and forbidding. The problem he saw was in deciding "how much to forbid, at what times and by what means."[5] The problem was compounded by taking into account the fact that children, pupils, "have very different innate constitutional dispositions, so that it is quite impossible that the same educational procedure can be equally good for all children."[6]

Freud's interest was in preventing the neurotic illness that certainly is related to the suppression of instinct, but he saw a danger in establishing a pedagogy based on the idea of freedom. Instead, he advised a balance between instinct and inhibition; he spoke for maintaining the tension between the forces of impulse and constraint. To achieve such a balanced focus, teachers need to have fairly refined skills of observing and inferring individual states of being. Hudson speaks to this view as well when he says:

> The danger, conceptually speaking, lies in establishing the idea of freedom as a simple and overriding criterion for deciding the day-to-day tactics of upbringing, rather than using it as a component of a more distant and more fundamental goal. Pursued literally, it leads to the denial of necessary tension and paradox, with results that can be both intellectually stultifying and downright nasty. Analogous consequences would seem to flow when we slip off the roof into the opposing gutter, and single-mindedly pursue the idea, not of freedom but of authority.[7]

The view of education I am proposing here includes room for developing good habits of inhibition without losing touch with one's impulses; it is a focus on percipient choosing, on purposeful postponement, on planning. In fact, having an interest and some skills in planning is a telling characteristic of most educated persons.

Nevertheless, since the nineteenth century and particularly during the 1960s, there have been educational theorists and teachers who celebrated the idea that freedom is better than forbiddance as a means of conducting classroom learning. From J. S. Mill's classical liberalism, through Tolstoy's anarchic individualism and Neill's radical psychoanalytic egalitarianism, and on to Rogers' person-centered psychology of self-actualization "non-interference" has been the watchword. Each of these figures proposes freedom as a means to meet the educational aims of, for example, positive self-esteem, investigative independence, and the "courage" to risk failing at unfamiliar tasks. They argue, and they are joined by John

Dewey on this point, that a child's own interest is the teacher's best guide in the facilitation of learning. This view also includes the belief that human nature (in children at least) is both independently oriented toward learning through the satisfaction of natural curiosity, and (Dewey drops out of the group here) that it is finally authoritative in matters of curriculum design (sequencing, integrating, synthesizing) and evaluation. The basic criterion for judging the success of such classroom operation is whether (and the degree to which) students are expressively engaged in some activity of whatever sort, so long as it is not destructive or hostile beyond acceptable limits.

The model on which this view is predicated comes from three familiar theoretical sources: (1) the egalitarian individualist[8] principle that all are (or should be, which is quite another matter) equal in social organizations as to their individual merits, or status, and as to their right to influence, judge, and constrain others; (2) the developmental principle that growth is a process of individual fulfillment which for its nourishment needs protection more than regulation, discipline, or deliberate shaping; and (3) the ethical principle of relativism which suggests that there is, in the end, no way to determine the appropriate criteria for settling differences about held values, and that each individual must determine his or her own set of values and the criteria for assessing their worth.

These principles of social egalitarianism, minimally inhibited individual development, and ethical relativism complement each other and constitute a view of freedom as a means in educational practice which has attracted a considerable number of supporters, especially among those who have entered the profession in recent years. It would seem that in order to criticize this position one would have to come out against equality, individualism, and a person's right to determine his or her own values. But this is not so. There are compelling arguments to be made against this view which do not require a rejection of equality, individualism, or the individual's right to determine personal values.[9]

If deliberate non-interference is the Scylla side of the problem of freedom's place in education, then Charybdis is represented by the rigid authoritarianism that is the deliberate frustration of individual wants and personal identity for the sake of an idea or a system that is made into a value that transcends individuals.

While few institutions exhibit a conscious preference for causing the frustration of individual impulse, education has produced enough such frustration in the past to raise the suspicion that educators do not see frustration itself as altogether harmful. The control of certain needs, the gratification of which is seen to be unacceptable—either on account of the long-term needs of the individual, or the larger needs of the social group in which the individual lives—seems to require suppression. And suppression frustrates. Psychologically speaking (and the pun is intended) suppression is forbidding. For those who acknowledge some value in suppression, frustration of impulse is at the heart of any structured educational experience.

The difficulty that educators must face is deciding how much of what sort of behavior to forbid and constrain. Too much frustration, or the wrong kind, produces neurotic maladaptations that are educational failures of the first order. Too little constraint on impulse produces an imbalance of id and ego which can inhibit psychological and intellectual development— insofar as that development is seen as balancing impulse and control, as mastering skills in social relations and rational judgment which will provide life-long possibilities for diverse satisfaction and safety.

Education then, as a prophylaxis against neurotic disease, and as the deliberate imposition of frustration in pursuit of skills, is a balancing act. There is always a danger of producing sociopathic alienation, or psychopathic neurosis through an extreme imbalance of either kind. The tension required to maintain the balance between impulse and inhibition is the protagonist of human biography. But civilization in general, and education in particular, has the effect of weakening instinct and impulse. That fact suggests the creation of an educational problem, a problem that has not been given adequate attention. The problem has two parts: (1) What should we teach the young about their own (weakened, but present) instincts? and (2) What should we teach the young that will help replace instinct as a means for getting on in social life?

Conflict, Communication, and Curriculum

Fifty years ago Freud published *Civilization and Its Discontents,* a book not normally associated with educational theory because education is mentioned directly only once—and then in a footnote. But the broad theme of the book, namely that civilization progresses as instinct gratification is delayed and even replaced by longer term arrangements for security, is of fundamental significance in educational theory. And the footnote itself makes a serious charge that education must answer:

> That education of young people at the present day conceals from them the part which sexuality will play in their lives is not the only reproach we are obliged to make against it. Its other sin is that it does not prepare them for the aggressiveness of which they are destined to become the objects. In sending the young out into life with such a false psychological orientation, education is behaving as though one were to equip people starting on a Polar expedition with summer clothing and maps of the Italian lakes.[10]

Schools then failed, and schools today still fail to teach what Freud considered basic and essential for human beings to know, even though schools are often given the public responsibility to prepare the children of the community for their own "Polar expeditions" in life. Freud goes on to point out an important ethical consideration that educators should be aware of:

In this [failure] it becomes evident that a certain misuse is being made of ethical demands. The strictness of those demands would not do so much harm if education were to say: "This is how men ought to be, in order to be happy and to make others happy; but you have to reckon on their not being like that." Instead of this the young are made to believe that everyone else fulfills those ethical demands—that is, that everyone else is virtuous. It is on this that the demand is based that the young, too, shall become virtuous.[11]

The fault is compounded. Schools initially fail to instruct students in the importance that sexuality and aggressiveness will have in their own lives, and then they create the impression that these fundamental attributes of human nature are not important or problematical in anyone's life—except perhaps in the degenerate and criminal. It is central to the argument of Freud's book that the development of civilization itself be understood as a reflection of the way in which impulses of this kind are handled. Nothing could be more basic and essential for getting on as social beings than understanding the bargains that must be struck between the immediate pleasure that comes from satisfaction of instincts, and the mediated sense of secure relations that comes from somehow dominating those instincts. In harsh terms, his view is that civilization makes progress by replacing pleasure with guilt, but education has done little to inform the young about what is happening to them, to help them to handle the guilt, and to explain why this tension is unavoidable and necessary in the development of civilized patterns of social relations.

Examined from this point of view, much of modern education is hard to defend. A lot of what is taught is neither basic nor essential for human beings as such, though it may be pleasant (e.g., music or modern fiction) and useful (e.g., electronics or English grammar), while most of what one might consider essential is either deliberately excluded from school curricula, or is overlooked through a negligent reluctance to consider such matters.

One of the interesting exceptions to this negligent attitude is the essay "Two Types of Teaching," published in 1965 by the British philosopher and educator John Wilson. In his essay, Wilson artfully argues a case for regarding certain skills of communication as essential to human beings as such, and therefore as subjects essential to a proper education.[12] This theme was soon to be elaborated in much of the "small group" and "open education" literature, but I shall use Wilson's essay to make my point because his statement of the theme is clear and unencumbered by the theoretical thicket that later grew over it.[13]

Wilson's plan for the essay is to imagine, "for a few glorious minutes," what we would do if we were "to educate human beings as human beings, for that part of our time at least which we [could] spare from the demands of society (many of which are of course quite reasonable)."[14] He tries to suspend all a priori assumptions about what students should be taught in order to become "cultured or civilized" and "good middle-class citizens." Instead he proposes to explore the question of what students themselves "*want* to be like, what they want to learn." Recognizing the vagueness that plagues such a question, Wilson nevertheless proceeds to speculate on behalf of these hypothetical students to the conclusion that "the ability to talk, walk, make friends, live at peace with your neighbours and express yourself sexually might be considered essential tools"[15] for satisfying basic wants and achieving happiness.

Wilson stresses that these tools are really skills, and the most important of these are the skills of communication. Learning "to communicate in certain ways" is the essential core of the education of human beings as human beings. Providing the milieu in which these skills can be learned and practiced is "the second type of teaching" which Wilson is trying to clarify. Being able to talk and listen with understanding are the basic skills, and they are difficult to teach.

People are frightened to speak, prejudiced, bewitched, over-eager, fanatical, and so forth. The difficulties can only be overcome by practice in small groups—run by a competent instructor. Herein lies the real problem: adults are not much better at talking than students.[16]

Wilson's view of what ought to be taught more closely re- sembles the view of a portrait than a wide-angle lens. He fo- cuses sharply on the needs of individuals and their close psychological context, but there is not much sociological or political depth of field. He does, however, make passing acknowledgement of the point Freud made about aggression:

> Without some degree of transference, identification, aggression and imitation no effective human education can be carried on. This, I think, is the basic truth that educators are reluctant to accept, even though parents have practiced it for millennia.[17]

Wilson's attention and his argument are confined primarily to establishing the importance of certain characteristics of the context of schooling in which such instruction might take place. All the same, Wilson's essay is important because it asks that crucial question about what is basic and essential for schools to be doing, and its answer is a sensible challenge to the current state of education.

Another and perhaps more significant exception to the neg- ligent attitude mentioned above is the program for teaching public issues in the high school developed by Donald Oliver and James Shaver.[18] They call their model a legal-ethical, or jurisprudential framework, and it is meant to emphasize "the clarification of two or more legitimately held points of view as they bear on a public policy question."[19] The authors argue (against the status quo of social studies curriculum) that con- temporary political controversy should be the major criterion for content selection and that the framework of issue analysis should be constructed from a view of pluralism that represents the value of human dignity as a right of all individuals.

Oliver and Shaver argue that a "plurality of active groups— that is, pluralism—is a necessary ingredient of a free society, because it is the only natural mechanism which can insure some freedom of choice."[20] And this insurance, they maintain, is necessary to the protection of human dignity. The authors present a conflict model of society as a means of portraying the realistic tensions that exist when individuals and groups are interdependent, as they are in a society that values pluralism.

> The position taken in this book is that for most of the public decisions required of a pluralistic society men cannot define truth in such unequivocal terms that all will see it and grasp it in the same way. The variety of backgrounds provided by the multiplicity of subgroups precludes this.[21]

On the basis of their position on pluralism Oliver and Shaver recommend that students "should be exposed to public problems within our society—situations over which individuals as well as the society are in conflict. And second, the student should be taught to analyze these public problems within some useful political and social framework."[22]

The framework that the authors have in mind is based on three important facts about human beings, facts that are indispensable to our understanding of how to get on decently with one another:

> First, each person is somehow different from all other people ... in what he believes, what he desires, ... thinks is good for himself, and how he feels about other people and other things in the world around him. Second, regardless of their individual differences, people generally choose to live in groups and modify some of their own personal desires and beliefs in order to get along with others who live in the same groups ... and depend upon one another for safety, shelter, and companionship. Third, the fact of being different and yet living in communities which face common problems leads to controversy and disagreement about decisions affecting the community.[23]

The framework is completed then with a procedure that the authors call "rational consent."

In this view, which represents the wide-angle frame as compared with Wilson's portrait close-up, the basic and indispensable terms are dignity (free choice), community, pluralism, political conflict, and rational consent. The idea is to teach students to confront conflict rather than avoid it, to respect legitimate differences and one's right to maintain them even in the face of conflict, and to seek rational consent to the means by which problems are to be solved. One could almost see the Oliver and Shaver program as a moderate and mild reply to Freud's accusation that the schools fail to prepare students for the tough going they will encounter with regard to aggression at least, if not sexuality.

A number of recent theorists in the sociology of education[24] have attempted to articulate a more radical framework for the analysis of schools and the knowledge, or "cultural capital," which the schools presumably control; their approach is a third exception to the negligent attitude described above. Using the capitalist economic structure as a metaphor, these works present a conception of knowledge and control—and a particular sort of educational hegemony—as fundamentally problematic in both an epistemological and a political sense. This very separation of "epistemological" and "political" would be a topic of great concern for these writers, because they see the very process of coming to know something as politically determined, in the same way as coming to own something is determined by certain economic and political controls. Michael Apple, author of a recent book on ideology and curriculum, describes his point of view this way:

As we learn to understand the way education acts in the economic sector of a society to reproduce important aspects of inequality, so too are we learning to unpack a second major sphere in which schooling operates. For not only is there economic property, there also seems to be symbolic property—cultural capital—which schools preserve and distribute. Thus, we can now begin to get a more thorough understanding of how institutions of cultural preservation and distribution like schools create and recreate

> forms of consciousness that enable social control to be maintained
> without the necessity of dominant groups having to resort to overt
> mechanisms of domination. Increasing our understanding of this
> recreation is at the heart of this volume.[25]

This neo-marxist language runs through much of the so-
called new sociology of education, further emphasizing its
political focus. The spokesmen of the new sociology ask how
students are taught what those who control the economy take
to be necessary for the protection of social and institutional
order, not what is basic and indispensable for the students
themselves to get on as decent people in modern social milieux.
As I suggested in Chapter 3, some of the work done from this
perspective (e.g., that of Basil Bernstein and Pierre Bourdieu)
holds promise for contributing to power theory.

Wilson's emphasis on the significant skills of personal communication, and the Oliver and Shaver jurisprudential model
of pluralist-rational conflict resolution are insufficient, in my
view (and here I agree with some of the new sociologists), to
overcome the hegemonic presumptions of public education and
its abetting of undemocratically concentrated power. The fact
remains that much of what young people need to know, as they
try to survive on their infirm instincts, is not considered education's business and must therefore be learned elsewhere, if it
is to be learned at all. This situation is particularly frustrating
when one recalls that our times are distinguished for inventing
the right for (almost) everyone to attend school and then transforming that right into an obligation sanctioned by compulsory
attendance laws. We now compel the sapping of instinct
through education, which is a civilizing mixture of activity and
postponement, information and taboo, individuation and organization, but we have not been careful enough in replacing
with knowledge what we have taken from nature.

Pluralism and Powerlessness

Oliver and Shaver have suggested that pluralism is both a
social value and a framework for social conflict analysis. But it

seems that as a society of many cultures, the United States has decided to insist on something very close to a uniform, universal (but no longer free) education on the grounds that such a provision would not only render individuals better off in the long run, but that it would render the society per se better off, too. That is the simple and fundamental ethical premise on which our system of public schooling was constructed. The emphasis in fact has been on the smallest unit, each individual person, and on the largest one, the society itself. We have traditionally put less emphasis on the middle-sized subcultures and local communities and, as a result, pluralism as a social ideal has been overshadowed in our schools by the ideal of "acculturation."[26]

American public schools have a long history of acculturation, but pluralism remains strong as a social value in spite of sustained organizational pressures to diminish it within the educational system. Perhaps pluralism's strength is attributable to the very diversity of people's aims, the acknowledgment of which means that we must live with the permanent possibility of conflict, even tragedy. Pluralism recognizes this condition as a truth and does not try to change it into the false harmony of acculturation; in so doing, pluralism becomes the more humane ideal.

Americans are divided now more than ever into groups that transcend the traditional class distinctions. It matters now, and it matters a great deal, how we identify people in terms that include ethnicity, sex, age, occupation, political affiliation, union affiliation, membership in social and service organizations, educational level, income, marital status, and so on. One's social identity, so to speak, is a composite of variables much more complex than the old "lower, middle, and upper," or, in Marx's terms, "working, bourgeois, and ruling," classes. Acculturation has become somewhat of a suspect ideal as emphasis has shifted to establishing and defending the legitimacy of individual and group differences. But no educational system can provide adequate means for the accommodation of all these differences, let alone their full development and celebration.

The tenacity of pluralism as a social ideal in America has quite successfully challenged the uniform acculturation aspects of universal education, but with the unhappy consequence that schools are trying to be too many things for too many different people without changing their basic ideas of what should be taught as necessary for life in a social world regardless of one's particular cultural affiliation or social identity. This is the critical curricular problem for educational theory.

But what does it mean to say that education ought to help provide what is basic and necessary for getting on with some decency in the social world? And how can this question be answered with due regard for the principle of pluralism but without thereby dissipating completely the informal assemblage of different cultures which is the unsteady nucleus of our society? How can education border, protect, and salute differences between individuals and among groups without causing the differing parties to break apart and go so far in their own separate ways that they no longer can see or understand each other—like the ships of a fleet that are slowly scattered by high shifting winds? How can education achieve the democratic ideal of linking without hobbling?

According to the severest critics of American education, we have achieved just the opposite of this ideal. We have not been able to link the people, groups, and cultures of the nation in a chain of cooperative relations, but we have managed to hobble the members of almost every "minority" category—not in spite of educational efforts, but (partly) because of them. Having failed to teach the skills and confidence necessary for self-government, and having failed to provide the conditions that make it possible for people to recognize their own social and political rights, the state now is obliged to take care of the ordinary people who apparently cannot take care of themselves.

These critics would say that public education actually undermines the political capacities of the many, and so acts as a partial solution to the problem of politically troublesome groups. They would argue that schooling is a kind of obedience training: its emphasis is on conforming to the rules, roles, and regulations of educational (and other) institutions, while there is no emphasis on learning to resist, on learning how to disagree successfully with those who hold positions of authority. The governing theme of this criticism is that schools do not teach skills; rather they teach an incapacity to resist. The upshot is that ordinary people cannot take care of themselves, the government steps in to lend a paternal hand, and in so doing the state establishes a new and more subtle kind of control over a huge number of dependent citizens. The state is presented as a greedy therapist who teaches clients to depend on him rather than to become independent—being helped becomes a way of life. This highly organized, professional, benevolent paternalism has come to be known as the new therapeutic state, and as an institution of major importance within the state, education is taken to be inherently therapeutic, too. The problem is an excessive professional domination of personal life.

As the web of government and its educational system(s) becomes more encompassing and more powerful, an increasing number of the people whom the government is supposed to represent, whom education is supposed to prepare for getting on decently and effectively in the social world, sense their powerlessness. For example, it was reported in the *New York Times*[27] that almost 100 million Americans over the age of eighteen did not vote in the 1978 elections. That is the lowest percentage (about one-third) of eligible voters to exercise their franchise since 1942. Curtis Gans, director of the Committee for the Study of the American Electorate, is quoted as saying:

> Our country's legitimacy is premised on the consent of the governed. And more and more of the governed are not lending their consent by not voting. In the long haul we could have a government of interested parties, organized interested parties.

It is apparent that many people, especially the young, feel powerless to make any difference in an election. A twenty-three-year-old New Jersey clerk was quoted in the same article as saying:

> Maybe when I get older and own a house of my own and pay taxes, I'll be more into society. We'll be taking over the country soon, and maybe I'll have more interest. But right now my parents, the adults, are in charge.

One of "the adults in charge" had this to say however, as she sat having her hair cut instead of voting:

> I really don't think there's much you can do about anything. It's getting to be frustrating. I'm just a little person who doesn't have much pull. But that's the way of the world, I guess.

Finally, this saddening sense of powerlessness was extended even to those elected in the end: "It doesn't matter who gets elected," said a nurse in Maryland. "They can't do what they want. They're controlled by the people around them. So it doesn't matter whether I vote."

The young don't vote because the adults are in charge. But the adults don't vote because they don't think it makes any difference to a given election, and even if it did make a difference the new officeholders would be controlled by "the people around them" anyway. This almost sounds like a belief in rule by Nobody, which is the most tyrannous form of government because there is no one to hold accountable.[28]

People who do not bother to act in a politically responsible way, who apparently have neither the skills nor the confidence necessary for participatory government, if not self-government, could be considered witnesses for the critics who say that public education actually undermines the political capacities of the many who have a learned incapacity to resist—or to assert. The powerlessness they sense subdues them into a most passive condition. But their passiveness is a form of consent, and the politicians know this.

This example of voting behavior is only one of many that

could provide a concrete image for what is a more abstract problem. The problem is that many "educated" people feel powerless and do not know how to act freely, that is, they do not have the skills of freedom. By "act freely" I mean being able to transform a future reference into the mechanics of possibility. This ability is a composite of several skills that can be taught and, in my way of thinking, ought to be taught in schools because the skills and the composite ability to act freely are basic and necessary for getting on in modern social life. These skills, together with an understanding of the idea of power in relation to powerlessness, would constitute the basis of a new ethics for the curriculum of public education. It is an ethics that is continuous with the proposals made by Wilson, Oliver, Shaver, and some of the new theory in the sociology of education, but it develops quite a different focus.

Returning to Freud's challenge for a moment, I would agree that some knowledge of the role that sexuality and aggression will play in their lives is essential for the education of the young. But I think Freud was more correct about sexuality, which has become a subject of wide public attention and controversy in the last few years, than he was about aggression. The reason for this is that I see aggression as but one form of a larger concept that is an aspect of all social relations that involve at least two people and a plan for action. That concept is power. Knowledge of power, along with the skills of freedom, are two of the most important pieces of equipment that each one of us needs for the "Polar expedition" of modern social life. These subjects are the foundations of moral education just as they are the conceptual cornerstones for educational practice and educational theory in a democratic design for social relations.

Power and the Skills of Freedom

I have suggested that any satisfactory answer to the question of what is basic and indispensable to teach in our society must emphasize the importance of knowing what power is and of obtaining the skills needed for acting freely. By helping to teach these two "subjects" education can contribute to the preservation of democratic institutions, the future of which depends on a broader distribution of power and a greater number of autonomous (self-governing) people. In the remaining pages I will summarize the analysis of power and the proposed logic of freedom, and then discuss some of the implications that follow for education and American society.

Power. First of all it must be recognized that power is a fundamental category of human experience—as fundamental to social science as energy is to physics. It is an aspect of all social life whenever at least two people are related through a plan for action—from parents and their children, to lovers, teachers and students, teammates, bosses and workers, doctors and patients, and all the way to tyrants and slaves.

Power is partly psychological because it requires a plan, an intention. It is partly social because it requires at least two people who are related in a particular way, and it is always found where organization is, whether in a family or a multinational corporation. And power is always instrumental because it is an action idea, a means in relation to a plan. Power is pragmatic.

All power is delegated and is maintained through the consent of those who delegate the power. There are several kinds of consent from acquiescence under threat of sanction, through compliance, indifference, and conformity, to commitment through informed judgment. The withdrawal of consent is the final power over power. Any power-holder is limited by the consent (good will) of those who delegate the power, and by the unpredictability of power's long-term effects.

The anti-power concept is not "morality" but instrumental insignificance. Both the moral and the immoral can use power—which is the ability to get others to help accomplish a plan.

Power is unavoidable in social life because power occurs wherever organization does, and social life is always organized somehow. But power does come in different forms. These are: (1) force, which is the most primitive, common, and unstable form; (2) fiction (in the sense of inventing and shaping a convenient assumption), which is a way of inducing consent by changing a belief; (3) finance (in the sense of providing some kind of reward for services), which is cost-benefit bargaining; and (4) fealty, which is a balanced and mutual trust close to love, and probably the most stable form of power.

There is no such thing as absolute power, if by that we mean power that is not accountable to anyone, because all power depends on consent.

The Logic of Freedom.   The term "freedom" is structurally ambiguous and essentially contestable, but one can argue persuasively for a current "best use."

All cases of freedom have both "free from" and "free to" attributes, and all cases have three necessary elements: P is free from O to do (be, have) X. In this formula, O stands for constraints. Constraints can be categorized by using the constraint matrix (see page 133); actual constraints can be sorted out from merely possible ones, those that are active from those that are abeyant, the psychobiological from the social from the equivocal. All of this is useful for reconceiving a problem of freedom into a form that makes clearer the relationship between one's intention and the relevant constraints on one's ability to realize that intention.

Skills in using this matrix to diagnose actual constraints are central to the ability to act freely. "Acting freely" means being able to transform a future reference into the mechanics of possibility.

A synonym for this sense of freedom is autonomy, which means self-governing, and which depends on the ability to establish a hierarchy of wants, values, and reasons. Autonomy is an achievement, not a given.

Like power, freedom is partly psychological (internal hierarchy of wants, values, reasons); partly social (freedom is a term of relation whose basic parts are you, me, and us, and it implies responsibility for actions taken); and instrumental (because freedom is always *for* something, and in that sense, all freedoms are means to other ends). Freedom is not valued for itself alone.

Freedom is a concept used to indicate the status of constraints that are relative to a plan for action. It is a concept with rational, relational, and diagnostic qualities joined together in the process of choosing and judging plans for action in a context of constraints.

Teaching Power and Freedom. Both power and freedom are fundamental categories of human experience. We often use freedom in one of its many senses to help explain other important terms and situations. I have tried to provide a somewhat novel view of freedom by placing great stress on a method of diagnosing the configuration of constraints particular to a given problem. I think that this method, and the matrix that represents it, will be useful in sorting out real problems of freedom in everyday life, and in teaching the skills of freedom.

Most people, and educators in particular, have not often used power to help explain other important terms and social relationships. I see this as a form of moralistic fallacy in the understanding of power, and have argued for a fresh understanding of power that is independent of its reputation as a "bad word." No one can avoid power in social relations; one can only avoid thinking about it and understanding it.

My analysis makes power teachable, too. It helps to explain the possibility of practice. As an aspect of all social relations that involve at least two people and a plan for action, power has a set of discernible characteristics and four distinct forms. These characteristics and forms can be identified, illustrated, explained, practiced—in short, they can be taught. And in order to achieve the democratic principle that requires a broad distribution of power, knowledge about power ought to be taught.

Clever teachers can use the forms of power (force, fiction, finance, and fealty) in their methods of teaching anything, and then reflect on the different effects caused by each. Of course, these forms can be used in teaching power itself, too. In any case, we should recognize that power already exists in the various social relations of the school, even though it does not yet exist as a focus of study. It should, and I have tried to demonstrate a way in which it can be taught.

Imagination and Autonomy

Both power and freedom have to do with what has not yet happened and, as such, any formulation of either concept implies some particular intent or plan. To make talk about power or freedom sensible one must make clear whose intention to do what is being constrained in which ways. To have an intention is to have a concern with a future that does not yet exist, but which one wants to bring about. It is also to have a concern with oneself. As Gordon Allport put it:

> Intentional characteristics represent above all else the individual's primary modes of addressing himself to the future. As such they select stimuli, guide inhibitions and choices, and have much to do with the process of adult becoming.[29]

Power and freedom have a good deal to do with personality and a person's own sense of self. A sense of time, a sense of self, and planned change are related. The sense of self which one develops depends on whether one can even imagine long-term goals and whether one can develop skills to do the possible. The development of imagination in turn depends on personal experiences, on the way one's family sees the future, and more generally it depends on certain salient features of the social systems in which we live. Benjamin Singer characterizes the relation between personality and time as the "future-focused role-image"; it is "our self-image projected into the future, and it lends meaning to much of what we do in the present."[30]

Singer makes a telling point about the effects of a poorly developed sense of self-in-the-future:

> The linkage of time, selfhood and change is particularly important in considering the problems of the poor, the ghettoized, the inhabitants of developing nations. For those whose future-focused role-image is diffuse are the very individuals who compensate by depending on "fate."[31]

Singer's is a good example of a problem of freedom which can be diagnosed in part as caused by an active equivocal constraint. This dependence on fate may be traced to an abeyant psychobiological constraint, namely, the inability to imagine a future for oneself. As paradoxical as it may sound, one remedy for this particular problem of freedom is to enrich the imagination. We need imagination to function and to survive; we need to dream to solve problems. That people learn to cope with their lives through imagination is a well-known psychiatric principle, but it is less well known as a principle of education or politics. A good question to ask about the relation of freedom, power, and imagination might be: What is the psychological, social, and political value of the world of fantasy, composed of familiar bits of reality put together in strange forms, and how does the imaginative process find its place in education?[32]

I would say that the ability to imagine a world put together in a way that does not exist (but is composed of remnants of reality) is very like the basic ability to plan. The language of imagination is the language of a world one *constructs,* a world that one *wants* to construct, and not the world as one sees it today. This is also the language of planning, of intending, when some means to bring about the imagined world is attached to the future reference. As I have argued, to act freely means to transform a future reference into the mechanics of possibility. The language of imagination is the language of freedom, too.

Depending on "fate" is not only a sign that one lacks the ability to imagine influencing a future for oneself, it is the antithesis of autonomy. Autonomy, in contrast to an impulse, or a dependence on "fate," is an *achievement*. It is a kind of mastery in the skills of governing. But what does "govern" mean? *Webster's New International Dictionary,* Second Edition, explains that the word comes from the Greek (and Sanskrit) for tiller, or carriage pole, and means to steer or pilot. Further, it means "to direct and control the actions or conduct of, either by established laws or by arbitrary will ... to regulate; influence; restrain; administer." As a general term, "govern" implies "direction, control, or restraint." As I have argued, freedom as autonomy is freedom through direction, control, and restraint. It has little to do with impulse and less to do with fate.

The skills of freedom then, if freedom is considered to be more like autonomy than anomie, would be the skills of directing, controlling, regulating, influencing, restraining, and administering. Speaking generally, all of these actions depend on imagination, foresight, planning, respect for evidence, control of information, and some understanding of organization. An autonomous person would be one who is able and disposed to conceive of circumstances that do not yet exist but are plausible, to make judgments based on evidence that is likely to bring about the desired change in circumstances; to alter a course of action as new evidence warrants; and to organize available resources to help accomplish the plan. (This last is the formula for power, too.)

Behind these applied skills lie two crucial features of autonomy: accurate perception of self and of relevant sources of information (gathering information); and accurate processes of inference (organizing and assessing information to produce judgment). These two features of autonomy are no less than the foundations of science and logic. The capacity to act freely, to be autonomous, would then seem to require some study of the various scientific methods of inquiry and the logical processes of reasoning to sound judgment. Skills in posing questions (imagining, hypothesizing), gathering and assessing information relevant to the question, and then posing a plan for action— these skills are at the core of modern education for freedom and for power. Education is preparation for the long-term. It should focus on enriching the imagination and on the skills of controlling information, for these are the means of survival we need to teach the young if they are to challenge fate at all.

Education must focus on the rudiments of freedom and power because it is a very risky business to leave their development to chance. It is just not realistic to suppose that inherent goodwill and decency in any society will insure and protect freedom from unreasonable constraints, nor will power and knowledge about power be distributed as broadly as possible unless someone sees to it. Freedom for the modern American depends on a capacity to resist the control by others which extends over daily life, but, as David Potter has argued, it depends now "more than ever on his own willpower and self-control. Eternal vigilance remains the price of liberty, but the first person to watch is oneself."[33]

Choice, Freedom, and Power

I have argued that the key to understanding power is in the nature of consent, and the key to understanding freedom is in diagnosing constraints. Maybe I should stop there, but I cannot resist a strong urge to suggest that the master key to understanding both power and freedom is choice. Not a mindless, willy-nilly opting for this or that, but *percipient* choice based on keen perception and mindful foresight. Choosing well needs intellect, it needs what Learned Hand called the "intolerable labor of thought." I would agree with Aristotle that "the origin of action—its efficient, not its final cause—is choice, and that of choice is desire and reasoning with a view to an end."[34]

Another way to state this point is to say that the capacity to make and vary plans, a capacity that includes the skills of imagination, observation, diagnosis, and judgment, is the basis of both power and freedom. Such capacity also includes a presumption that one is able to overcome the mordant hostility toward organizational management that is the mark of so many otherwise educated minds. An understanding of organization is essential to an understanding of power—and to every fundamental aspect of civilized society. Freedom becomes an *ideal* because people are frustrated and because they feel dominated by "organization," but when freedom is made into such an ideal it is placed in a false dichotomy with organization and loses its effect as an instrument for achieving other social values.

Deep in the center of my own notions of education lie two principal activities—the play of imagination in generating visions of what might be, and the work of controlling such information as we have been able to produce and gather together over generations.

If we can learn to think of freedom as a habit of intelligent (imaginative) foresight, then we can think of ourselves as being pulled by choices rather than pushed by antecedent determinants. Power and freedom can be conceived as the means needed for acting out plans for changing the world as we see it into the world as we are able to imagine it. This conception is the basis of a revised ethics of education.

The philosophy of power developed in this book can be taken as an answer to the problem of force and to the threat of an absolute power. We must teach all the forms of power, and we must be certain that we teach the nature of consent. It is important to any understanding of this view that one has some successful experience in disagreeing with authority, so that the dynamics of delegation and consent are lived out. It is important, too, that the young experience their own (relative) powerlessness but with the guidance that will help them to understand it. Power and powerlessness, like sexuality and aggression, are facts of life for which the young need preparation.

Education should help to expose the coercive effects of subtle and impersonal uses of power, otherwise they will thrive in the shadows created by our tendency to reject the topic of power out of fright. We must teach, too, that freedom is less a remote ideal and more a set of rational skills. Freedom, like personality, is an achievement that requires much "intolerable labor of thought." Many will resist this idea, as many have. Then as the oppressive consequences of escaping this labor close in on their lives, they will wonder why they are not even able to imagine what they want, or to do anything effective about getting it.

We cannot teach the skills of freedom by letting the young do whatever they want and express themselves however they wish for as long as they like. Although emotion is a very important part of everyone's life, and individuality ought in many cases to be encouraged, neither has a great deal to do with the skills of freedom—and that is why I have not digressed to discuss them at any length.

Nor can we teach power merely by pointing a finger at its densest concentrations and most flagrant abuses and then wagging our heads in moral dismay. We must examine power and powerlessness in everyday relations, in our own lives, and learn to teach it from the inside out. We must help the young experience the forms of power knowledgeably and so improve our chances of moving away from force and closer to love. Away from the powerlessness of isolated, competitive individualism and closer to the cooperative linkage with others which is the basis of democratic organization, and the basis of power.

Notes

Introduction: Rethinking the Obvious

1. Sigmund Freud, *Group Psychology and the Analysis of the Ego* (New York: Liveright, 1922), p. 39.

2. Among the volumes surveyed were: *The Encyclopaedia Britannica* (both the 11th and 15th editions); *Dictionary of the History of Ideas* (P. P. Wiener, ed.); *Ballantine's Law Dictionary; The Encyclopedia of Philosophy* (P. Edwards, ed.); *Dictionary of Philosophy* (D. D. Runes, ed.); *Encyclopaedia of Religion and Ethics* (J. Hastings, ed.); *A Dictionary of Politics* (W. Z. Laqueur, ed.); *Dictionary of Political Science* (J. Dunner, ed.); *A Dictionary of Sociology* (G. D. Mitchell, ed.); *A Dictionary of the Social Sciences* (J. Gould and W. L. Kolb, eds.); *Encyclopaedia of the Social Sciences* (E. R. A. Seligman, ed.); *Dictionary of Behavioral Science* (B. B. Wolman, ed.); *The Encyclopedia of Human Behavior* (R. M. Goldenson, ed.); *Encyclopedia of Psychology* (H. J. Eysenck, W. Arnold, and R. Meili, eds.); *Encyclopedia of Psychoanalysis* (L. Eidelberg, ed.); *The Encyclopedia of Mental Health* (A. Deutsch, ed.); *Encyclopedia of Educational Research* (R. L. Ebel, ed.); *The Encyclopedia of Education* (F. C. Deighton, ed.); *Dictionary of Education* (C. V. Good, ed.); *Handbook of Research on Teaching* (both 1st and 2d editions); and *The Encyclopedia of Management* (C. Heyel, ed.).

3. *Dictionary of Behavioral Science,* p. 285.

4. *Dictionary of Sociology,* p. 227.

5. *A Modern Dictionary of Sociology,* p. 307.

6. W. J. McCallister, *The Growth of Freedom in Education,* 2 vols. (Port Washington, N.Y.: Kennikat Press, 1971), 1, p. 1.

7. Frithjof Bergmann, *On Being Free* (Notre Dame: University of Notre Dame Press, 1977), p. 1.

8. For a discussion of how federal and state regulations have come to control the public school curriculum in the last twenty years, see J. Myron Atkin, "The Government in the Classroom," *Daedalus* (Summer 1980), pp. 85–97.

1. The Prominent Ambivalence of Power in America

1. D. C. McClelland, J. W. Atkinson, R. A. Clark, and E. L. Lowell, *The Achievement Motive* (New York: Appleton, 1953); D. C. McClelland, *The Achieving Society* (Princeton: Van Nostrand, 1961).

2. Two recent books on this are: David Winter, *The Power Motive* (New York: Free Press, 1973); and D. C. McClelland, *Power: The Inner Experience* (New York: Irvington, 1975).

3. Power as a defense mechanism—through identification with the aggressor—has been discussed in the works of Anna Freud and Bruno Bettelheim.

4. Dorwin Cartwright, "Power: A Neglected Variable in Social Psychology," in *Studies in Social Power,* ed. Dorwin Cartwright (Ann Arbor: University of Michigan, Research Center for Group Dynamics, 1959), p. 2. There are many useful papers in this collection.

5. Ibid., p. 2.

2. The Very Idea of Power

1. Lord Acton (J. E. E. Dahlberg-Acton), *Essays on Freedom and Power* (Boston: Beacon Press, 1948), p. 364.

2. Rollo May, *Power and Innocence: A Search for the Sources of Violence* (New York: Norton, 1972).

3. Edgar Z. Friedenberg, *Coming of Age in America* (New York: Random House, 1965), pp. 47–48.

4. Many stipulative definitions have been offered; here are a few interesting examples: Thomas Hobbes, *Leviathan* (Baltimore: Penguin, 1968), p. 150—"The Power of a Man, (to take it Universally,) is his present means, to attain some future apparent Good." Bertrand Russell, *Power* (New York: Norton, 1938), p. 35—"Power may be defined as the production of intended effects." Harold D. Lasswell and Abraham Kaplan, *Power and Society* (New Haven: Yale University Press, 1950), p. 76—"Power is a special case of the exercise of influence: it is the process of affecting policies of others with the help of

(actual or threatened) severe deprivations for nonconformity with the policies intended." Adolph A. Berle, *Power* (New York: Harcourt, Brace and World, 1969), p. 37, offers five "natural laws" of power: (1) power invariably fills any vacuum in human organization; (2) it is invariably personal; (3) it is always based on a system of ideas; (4) it is exercised through institutions; and (5) it is invariably confronted with a field of responsibility. Peter Nettl, "Power and the Intellectuals," in *Power and Consciousness,* eds. Conor Cruise O'Brien and W. D. Vanech (New York: New York University Press, 1969), p. 17—"By power I simply mean something that causes the restructuring of action without altering preferences; you are made to do something irrespective of whether it is your preferred course of action." Rollo May, *Power and Innocence* (New York: Norton, 1972), p. 99—"Power is the ability to cause or prevent change."

5. Bertrand Russell, *Power: A New Social Analysis* (New York: Norton, 1938), p. 12.

6. Ibid., pp. 13–14.

7. Ibid., p. 35.

8. David Winter, *The Power Motive* (New York: Free Press, 1973).

9. D. C. McClelland, *Power: The Inner Experience* (New York: Irvington, 1975).

10. For further discussion of love, see Robert C. Hazo, *The Idea of Love* (New York: Praeger, 1967); Douglas N. Morgan, *Love: Plato, the Bible and Freud* (Englewood Cliffs, N.J.: Prentice-Hall, 1964); and Thomas Gould, *Platonic Love* (New York: Free Press, 1963).

11. Robert Michels, *Political Parties* (New York: Free Press, 1949).

12. Hannah Arendt, *On Violence* (New York: Harcourt, Brace and World, 1970), p. 38.

13. Ibid., pp. 38–39.

14. Plato, *Republic,* bk. VIII: 563ff.

15. See Charles E. Merriam, *Political Power* (New York: Collier Books, 1964), chapter 6.

16. Étienne de la Boétie, *The Politics of Obedience: The Discourse of Voluntary Servitude* (New York: Free Life Editions, 1975), p. 46.

17. Ibid., p. 59.

18. Hannah Arendt, *Eichmann in Jerusalem* (New York: Viking, 1965), pp. 287–288.

19. Stanley Milgram, *Obedience to Authority* (New York: Harper and Row, 1974).

20. Ibid., p. 3.

21. Ibid., p. 4.

22. Ibid., p. 21.

23. Ibid., p. 5.

24. Adolph A. Berle, *Power* (New York: Harcourt, Brace and World, 1969), pp. 66–67.

25. Quoted in W. H. Auden and Louis Kronenberger, eds., *The Viking Book of Aphorisms* (New York: Viking, 1966), p. 301.

3. *Power and Education*

1. A. Czartoryski, *Education for Power* (London: Davis-Poynter, 1975), p. 111.

2. Basil Bernstein, "Education Cannot Compensate for Society," *New Society* (26 February 1970), p. 347.

3. *Gorgias,* 466 *et seq.*

4. Werner Jaeger, *Paideia,* 3 vols. (New York: Oxford University Press, 1943), 2, pp. 133–134.

5. Bertrand Russell quipped, after publishing his first book of short stories (*Satan in the Suburbs*), "I have devoted the first eighty years of my life to philosophy, and propose to devote the next eighty years to another branch of fiction." Quoted on the back cover of Barry Feinberg, ed., *The Collected Stories of Bertrand Russell* (New York: Simon and Schuster, 1972).

6. See Peter M. Blau, *Exchange and Power in Social Life* (New York: Wiley, 1964); Brian Barry, ed., *Power and Political Theory* (New York: Wiley, 1976); U. G. Foa and E. B. Foa, *Societal Structures of the Mind* (Springfield, Ill.: C. C. Thomas, 1974).

7. Philip W. Jackson, *Life in Classrooms* (New York: Holt, Rinehart, and Winston, 1968), p. 26.

8. Ibid., p. 22.

9. Ibid., p. 102.

10. Carl R. Rogers, *Freedom to Learn* (Columbus, Ohio: Charles E. Merrill, 1969), pp. 103–115.

11. Carl R. Rogers, *On Personal Power: Inner Strength and Its Revolutionary Impact* (New York: Delacorte, 1977).

12. See Steven Lukes, *Power: A Radical View* (London: Macmillan, 1974).

13. Dan C. Lortie, *Schoolteacher: A Sociological Study* (Chicago: University of Chicago Press, 1975), p. 102.

14. Ibid., p. 102. Emphasis in the original.

15. R. S. Peters, *Ethics and Education* (London: Allen and Unwin, 1976), p. 239.

4. *"Lyberte or Freedome Is a Mouche Swete Thynge"*

1. The title comes from a Middle English translation of Aesop. See *Caxton's Aesop,* ed. R. T. Lenaghan (Cambridge, Harvard University Press, 1967). Parts of this chapter first appeared as an essay called "Ambiguity and Constraint in the 'Freedom' of Free Schools," in *Ethics and Educational Policy,* ed. K. Strike and K. Egan (London: Routledge & Kegan Paul, 1978).

2. I. A. Richards, *How to Read a Page* (Boston: Beacon Press, 1959), p. 22.

3. Ibid., p. 24.

4. Felix Oppenheim, *Dimensions of Freedom* (New York: St. Martin's, 1961), p. 113.

5. J. S. Mill, *On Liberty* (New York: Appleton-Century-Crofts, 1947), p. 10.

6. Carl J. Friedrich, *An Introduction to Political Theory* (New York: Harper and Row, 1967), p. 25.

7. Ibid., p. 6.

8. David M. Potter, *Freedom and its Limitations in American Life* (Stanford: Stanford University Press, 1976), p. 61.

9. Ibid., p. 51.

10. Oppenheim, p. 147.

11. W. B. Gallie, "Essentially Contested Concepts," in *Proceedings of the Aristotelian Society,* 56 (1955–56), pp. 167–198.

12. Ibid., p. 169.

13. Ibid., pp. 171–172.

14. Ibid., p. 193.

15. Ralph Waldo Emerson, "Self-Reliance," in *The Selected Writings of Ralph Waldo Emerson,* ed. Brooks Atkinson (New York: Modern Library, 1950), p. 152.

16. Ibid., pp. 148–158.

17. George B. Hill and L. F. Powell, eds. *Boswell's Life of Johnson,* 6 vols. (Oxford: Clarendon Press, 1934), 2, p. 82.

18. B. F. Skinner, *Beyond Freedom and Dignity* (New York: Knopf, 1971).

19. Jonathan Kozol, *Free Schools* (Boston: Houghton Mifflin, 1972), p. 56.

20. Ibid., p. 50.

21. Paul Goodman, "Freedom and Learning: The Need for Choice," *Saturday Review* (18 May 1968), p. 73.

22. Ibid., p. 74.

23. Carl R. Rogers, *Freedom to Learn* (Columbus, Ohio: Charles E. Merrill, 1969), pp. 268–269.

24. Kozol, p. 11.

25. Matthew Arnold, *Culture and Anarchy* (London: Cambridge University Press, 1957), pp. 50, 74.

26. From *The Onion Eaters* by J. P. Donleavy, Copyright © 1971 by J. P. Donleavy. Used by permission of Delacorte Press/Seymour Lawrence.

27. For a helpful discussion of these issues see Hugh Petrie, "That's Just Einstein's Opinion: The Autocracy of Students' Reason in Open Education," in *The Philosophy of Open Education,* ed. David Nyberg (London: Routledge & Kegan Paul, 1975), pp. 61–78.

28. John Gardner, *Grendel* (New York: Knopf, 1971), p. 157.

29. Ludwig Wittgenstein, *Philosophical Investigations* (New York: Macmillan, 1953), p. 47e.

30. Ludwig Feuerbach, *The Essence of Christianity* (New York: Ungar, 1957), p. 17.

31. Bertell Ollman, *Alienation* (London: Cambridge University Press, 1971), p. 202.

32. Sigmund Freud, *Civilization and Its Discontents* (New York: Norton, 1962).

33. Mortimer J. Adler, *The Idea of Freedom,* 2 vols. (New York: Doubleday, 1958), 1, p. 617.

5. *The Skills of Freedom*

1. Jean-Jacques Rousseau, *Émile* (London: Everyman's Library, 1977), p. 56.

2. C. S. Lewis, *The Abolition of Man* (New York: Macmillan, 1947), pp. 47–48.

3. John Dewey, "Philosophies of Freedom," in his *Philosophy and Civilization* (New York: G. P. Putnam, 1931), pp. 278–279.

4. Ibid., p. 281.

5. Paul Weiss, *Man's Freedom* (New Haven: Yale University Press, 1950).

6. Joel Spring, *A Primer of Libertarian Education* (New York: Free Life Editions, 1975), p. 76.

7. George Gallup, *The Gallup Polls of Attitudes toward Education, 1969–1978* (Bloomington: *Phi Delta Kappa,* 1978).

8. Joel Feinberg, "The Idea of a Free Man," in *Educational Judg-*

ments, ed., James F. Doyle (London: Routledge & Kegan Paul, 1973), pp. 143–169.

9. George A. Kelly, *The Psychology of Personal Constructs,* 2 vols. (New York: Norton, 1955), vol. 1.

10. This distinction was brought out in a conversation on the matrix with Professor Jonas Soltis of Teachers College, Columbia University.

11. See Richard Kluger's *Simple Justice* (New York: Knopf, 1976).

12. Sophocles, *Antigone,* trans. Elizabeth Wyckoff (Chicago: University of Chicago Press, 1954), ii, 451–460.

13. Franz Kafka, *The Trial,* trans. Willa and Edwin Muir (New York: Knopf, 1937), pp. 57–58.

14. Max Kaltenmark, *Lao Tzu and Taoism* (Stanford: Stanford University Press, 1969), pp. 40–42.

15. It should be noted that Thoreau built his solitary hut less than a mile from his mother's house, which he continued to visit daily—velvet cushions and all.

16. Herbert Kaufman, *Red Tape: Its Origins, Uses, and Abuses* (Washington: The Brookings Institution, 1977), pp. 30 ff.

17. Ibid., pp. 58–59.

18. I am reminded of the story of a farmer whose neighbor saw him confronted with the bewildering complexity of the inner workings of a huge harvester that happened not to be working properly at the time. The neighbor asked his farmer friend whether he had ever worked on such a machine before. The answer was no. He asked whether the farmer knew what was wrong. Again, the answer was no. Finally, he asked the farmer how in the world he expected to fix the strange and intricate and enormous machine if he didn't know anything about it, and didn't know what was wrong with it. The farmer replied: "Well, it was made by a man, so I figure a man ought to be able to fix it."

19. Albert Camus, *The Myth of Sisyphus,* trans. Justin O'Brien (New York: Knopf, 1955), p. 20.

20. Ibid., p. 30.

21. Ibid., p. 14.

22. Ibid., p. 40.

23. Dewey, p. 297.

6. *Power and the Skills of Freedom*

1. For a good summary of current theory in moral education see David Purpel and Kevin Ryan, eds., *Moral Education* (Berkeley:

McCutchan, 1976), and Thomas Lickona, ed., *Moral Development and Behavior* (New York: Holt, Rinehart and Winston, 1976).

2. See, for example, Daniel Bell, *The Coming of Post-Industrial Society* (New York: Basic Books, 1976).

3. Liam Hudson, *Human Beings: The Psychology of Human Experience* (Garden City, N.Y.: Anchor, 1975), p. 158.

4. Sigmund Freud, *The Complete Introductory Lectures on Psychoanalysis* (New York: Norton, 1966), p. 613.

5. Ibid., p. 613.

6. Ibid., p. 613.

7. Hudson, pp. 167–168.

8. When the idea of society is rejected in favor of an every-individual-is-unique egoism, as in the thought of Max Stirner, for example, the egalitarian-individualist principle is referred to as the anarchist-individualist principle.

9. See Chapter 4.

10. Sigmund Freud, *Civilization and Its Discontents* (New York: Norton, 1962), p. 81.

11. Ibid., p. 81.

12. John Wilson, "Two Types of Teaching," in *Philosophical Analysis and Education*, R. D. Archambault, ed. (London: Routledge & Kegan Paul, 1965).

13. For a range of analytic essays on this see *The Philosophy of Open Education*, David Nyberg, ed. (London: Routledge & Kegan Paul, 1975).

14. Wilson, p. 158.

15. Ibid., p. 160.

16. Ibid., p. 165.

17. Ibid., p. 168.

18. Donald W. Oliver and James P. Shaver, *Teaching Public Issues in the High School* (Boston: Houghton Mifflin, 1966).

19. Ibid., p. 115.

20. Ibid., p. 10.

21. Ibid., p. 13.

22. Ibid., p. 13.

23. Ibid., p. 56.

24. See for example Jerome Karabel and A. H. Halsey, eds., *Power and Ideology in Education* (New York: Oxford University Press, 1977); and Michael F. D. Young, ed., *Knowledge and Control* (London: Collier-Macmillan, 1971).

25. Michael W. Apple, *Ideology and Curriculum* (London: Routledge & Kegan Paul, 1979), p. 3.

26. For a discussion of this see my "Education as Community Expression," *Teachers College Record,* 79 (1977), pp. 203–223; and W. Greenbaum, "America in Search of a New Ideal: An Essay on the Rise of Pluralism," *Harvard Educational Review,* 44 (1974), pp. 411–440.

27. "The Nonvoters: A Mood of Confusion and Pessimism," *New York Times,* 11 November 1978.

28. See above, pp. 44–45.

29. Gordon Allport, *Becoming* (New Haven: Yale University Press, 1955), p. 89.

30. Benjamin D. Singer, "The Future-Focused Role-Image," in *Learning for Tomorrow,* Alvin Toffler, ed. (New York: Vintage, 1974), p. 21.

31. Ibid., p. 22.

32. See Northrop Frye, *The Educated Imagination* (Bloomington: Indiana University Press, 1964), for a witty and stimulating discussion on this theme.

33. David M. Potter, *Freedom and Its Limitations in American Life* (Stanford: Stanford University Press, 1976), p. 61.

34. Aristotle, *Nicomachean Ethics,* 1139a.

Selected Bibliography

The following is a selection of books and articles that have enriched my own thinking about power, freedom, and education. It may be useful as a guide for the teacher who wishes to pursue the literature on these concepts.

Acton, Lord (J. E. E. Dahlberg-Acton). *Essays on Freedom and Power.* Boston: Beacon Press, 1948.

Adler, Alfred, *The Individual Psychology of Alfred Adler.* Eds. H. L. Ansbacher and R. R. Ansbacher. New York: Basic Books, 1956.

———. "The Psychology of Power." *Journal of Individual Psychology,* 22 (1966), pp. 166–172.

Adler, Mortimer J. *The Idea of Freedom.* 2 vols. New York: Doubleday, 1958, 1961.

Adorno, T. W., et al. *The Authoritarian Personality.* New York: Harper and Row, 1950.

Alinsky, Saul. *Rules for Radicals.* New York: Random House, 1971.

Allison, Lincoln. "The Nature of the Concept of Power." *European Journal of Political Research,* 2, no. 2 (1974), pp. 131–142.

Anshen, Ruth Nanda, ed. *Freedom: Its Meaning.* New York: Harcourt, Brace and Co., 1940.

Anton, Thomas J. "Power, Pluralism and Local Politics." *Administrative Science Quarterly,* 7 (1962), pp. 425–457.

Apple, Michael W., *Ideology and Curriculum.* London: Routledge & Kegan Paul, 1979.

Arendt, Hannah. *Eichmann in Jerusalem.* New York: Viking, 1965.

———. *On Violence.* New York: Harcourt, Brace and World, 1970.

Aron, Raymond. *An Essay on Freedom.* New York: New American Library, 1970.

Bachrach, Peter and Morton S. Baratz. *Power and Poverty.* New York: Oxford University Press, 1970.

———. "The Two Faces of Power." *American Political Science Review,* 56 (1962), pp. 947–952.

Ball, Terence. "Models of Power: Past and Present." *Journal of the History of the Behavioral Sciences,* 11, no. 3 (1975), pp. 211–222.

———. "Power, Causation and Explanation." *Polity,* 8, no. 2 (1975), pp. 189–214.

Barry, Brian, ed. *Power and Political Theory.* New York: Wiley, 1976.

Bay, Christian. *The Structure of Freedom.* Stanford: Stanford University Press, 1958.

Bazelon, David T. *Power in America.* New York: New American Library, 1967.

Bell, David V. J. *Power, Influence, and Authority.* New York: Oxford University Press, 1975.

Bergmann, Frithjof. *On Being Free.* Notre Dame: Notre Dame University Press, 1977.

Berle, Adolph A. *Power.* New York: Harcourt, Brace and World, 1969.

Berlin, Isaiah. *Four Essays on Liberty.* London: Oxford University Press, 1969.

———. "The Question of Machiavelli." *The New York Review of Books,* (November 4, 1971), pp. 20–32.

Bierstedt, Robert. *Power and Progress: Essays on Sociological Theory.* New York: McGraw-Hill, 1974.

Blau, Peter M. *Exchange and Power in Social Life.* New York: Wiley, 1964.

Bradshaw, Alan. "A Critique of Steven Lukes' *Power: A Radical View.*" *Sociology,* 10, no. 1 (1976), pp. 121–127.

Burns, James MacGregor. *Leadership.* New York: Harper and Row, 1978.

Canetti, Elias. *Crowds and Power.* New York: Viking, 1962.

Cartwright, D., ed. *Studies in Social Power.* Ann Arbor: Research Center for Group Dynamics, University of Michigan, 1959.

——— and A. Zander, eds. *Group Dynamics: Research and Theory.* New York: Harper and Row, 1968.

Champlin, John R. "On the Study of Power." *Politics and Society,* 1 (1970), pp. 91–111.

———, ed. *Power.* New York: Atherton, 1971.

Chesler, Mark A. and D. Worden. "Persistent Problems in 'Power and

Social Change.'" *The Journal of Applied Behavioral Science,* 10, no. 3 (1974), pp. 462-472.

Clegg, Stewart. *Power, Rule, and Domination.* London: Routledge & Kegan Paul, 1975.

———. *The Theory of Power and Organization.* London: Routledge & Kegan Paul, 1979.

Coleman, James S. "Loss of Power." *American Sociological Review,* 38 (1973), pp. 1-17.

———. *Power and the Structure of Society.* New York: Norton, 1974.

Cranston, Maurice. *Freedom.* New York: Basic Books, 1967.

Crick, B. "Freedom as Politics." *Philosophy, Politics and Society.* 3d series. Eds. P. Laslett and W. G. Runciman. London: Oxford University Press, 1967.

Crozier, Michael. "The Problem of Power." *Social Research,* 40, no. 2 (1973), pp. 211-228.

Dahl, Robert A. "The Concept of Power." *Behavioral Science,* 2 (1957), pp. 201-215.

———. *Modern Political Analysis.* 2d ed. Englewood Cliffs, N.J.: Prentice-Hall, 1970.

———. "Power." *International Encyclopedia of the Social Sciences.* Ed. David L. Sills. New York: Macmillan, 1968, vol. 12, pp. 405-415.

DeCrespigny, Anthony. "Power and its Forms." *Political Studies,* 16, no. 2 (1968), pp. 192-205.

D'Entrèves, Alexander Passerin. *The Notion of the State.* Oxford: Oxford University Press, 1967.

Dewey, John. *Freedom and Culture.* New York: Capricorn Books, 1963.

———. *Human Nature and Conduct.* New York: Modern Library, 1957.

———. *On Experience, Nature and Freedom.* Ed. R. J. Bernstein. Indianapolis: Bobbs-Merrill/The Library of Liberal Arts, 1960.

Djilas, Milovan. *The New Class.* New York: Praeger, 1957.

Domhoff, G. W. and H. B. Ballard, eds. *C. Wright Mills and the Power Elite.* Boston: Beacon Press, 1968.

Emerson, Ralph Waldo. *The Selected Writings of Ralph Waldo Emerson.* Ed. Brooks Atkinson. New York: Modern Library, 1950.

Emmet, Dorothy. "The Concept of Power." *Proceedings of the Aristotelian Society,* 54 (1953-54), pp. 1-26.

Etzioni, Amitai. *A Comparative Analysis of Complex Organizations.* 2d ed. New York: The Free Press, 1975.

Feinberg, Joel. "The Idea of a Free Man." *Educational Judgments: Papers in the Philosophy of Education.* Ed. James F. Doyle. London: Routledge & Kegan Paul, 1973.

——. *Social Philosophy*. Englewood Cliffs, N.J.: Prentice-Hall, 1973.

Foa, Uriel G. and Edna B. Foa. *Societal Structures of the Mind*. Springfield, Ill.: Charles C. Thomas, 1974.

Freud, Sigmund. *Civilization and Its Discontents*. New York: Norton, 1962.

Fromm, Erich. *Escape from Freedom*. New York: Holt, Rinehart and Winston, 1941.

Frye, Northrop. *The Educated Imagination*. Bloomington: Indiana University Press, 1964.

Gallie, W. B. "Essentially Contested Concepts." *Proceedings of the Aristotelian Society,* 56 (1955–56), pp. 167–198.

Gewirth, Alan. "Morality and Autonomy in Education." *Educational Judgments: Papers in the Philosophy of Education*. Ed. James F. Doyle. London: Routledge & Kegan Paul, 1973.

Gibson, Quentin. "Power." *Philosophy of the Social Sciences,* 1, no. 2 (1971), pp. 101–112.

Giddens, Anthony. "'Power' in the Recent Writings of Talcott Parsons." *Sociology,* 2, no. 3 (1968), pp. 257–272.

Gillam, Richard, ed. *Power in Postwar America*. Boston: Little, Brown, 1971.

Goodman, Paul. "Freedom and Learning: The Need for Choice," *Saturday Review,* (18 May, 1968).

——. *People or Personnel: Decentralizing and the Mixed System*. New York: Random House, 1965.

Gouldner, Alvin W., ed. *Studies in Leadership*. New York: Russell and Russell, 1965.

Haley, J. *The Power Tactics of Jesus Christ and Other Essays*. New York: Grossman, 1969.

Hickson, D. J. *et al.* "A Strategic Contingencies' Theory of Intraorganizational Power." *Administrative Science Quarterly,* 16, no. 2 (1971), pp. 216–229.

Hobbes, Thomas. *Leviathan*. New York: Penguin, 1968.

Hook, Sidney. *The Paradoxes of Freedom*. Berkeley: University of California Press, 1962.

Hudson, Liam. *Human Beings: The Psychology of Human Experience*. Garden City, N.Y.: Anchor, 1975.

Jaeger, Werner. *Paideia: The Ideals of Greek Culture*. 3 vols. London: Oxford University Press, 1944.

Jamieson, David W. and Kenneth W. Thomas. "Power and Conflict in the Student-Teacher Relationship." *The Journal of Applied Behavioral Science,* 10, no. 3 (1974), pp. 321–336.

Jouvenel, Bertrand de. *On Power*. Boston: Beacon Books, 1962.

Karabel, Jerome and A. H. Halsey, eds. *Power and Ideology in Education*. New York: Oxford University Press, 1977.

Kaufman, Herbert. *Red Tape: Its Origins, Uses, and Abuses*. Washington: The Brookings Institution, 1977.

Kinkade, Kathleen. "Power and the Utopian Assumption." *The Journal of Applied Behavioral Science*, 10, no. 3 (1974), pp. 402–414.

Kipnis, David. *The Powerholders*. Chicago: University of Chicago Press, 1976.

Kozol, Jonathan. *Free Schools*. Boston: Houghton Mifflin, 1972.

La Boétie, Étienne de. *The Politics of Obedience: The Discourse of Voluntary Servitude*. New York: Free Life Editions, 1975 (c. 1552).

Lasswell, Harold D. *Power and Personality*. New York: Norton, 1948.

—— and Abraham Kaplan. *Power and Society: A Framework for Political Inquiry*. New Haven: Yale University Press, 1950.

Lewis, C. S. *Studies in Words*. London: Cambridge University Press, 1960.

Lippett, R. *et al.* "The Dynamics of Power." *Human Relations*, 5 (1952), pp. 37–64.

Lortie, Dan C. *Schoolteacher: A Sociological Study*. Chicago: University of Chicago Press, 1975.

Lukes, Steven. *Power: A Radical View*. London: Macmillan, 1974.

——. "Reply to Bradshaw." *Sociology*, 10, no. 1 (1976), pp. 129–132.

McCallister, W. J. *The Growth of Freedom in Education: A Critical Interpretation of Some Historical Views*. 2 vols: Glasgow: Glasgow University Press, 1931; rpt. Port Washington, N.Y.: Kennikat Press, 1971.

MacCallum, Gerald C., Jr. "Negative and Positive Freedom." *The Philosophical Review*, 76 (July 1967), pp. 312–334.

McClelland, David C. *Power: The Inner Experience*. New York: Irvington, 1975.

McFarland, Andrew S. *Power and Leadership in Pluralist Systems*. Stanford: Stanford University Press, 1969.

Machiavelli, Niccolò. *The Prince*. New York: Norton, 1977.

MacIver, Robert M. "The Meaning of Liberty and Its Perversion." *Freedom, Its Meaning*. Ed. Ruth Nanda Anshen. New York: Harcourt, Brace and Co., 1940.

——. *Power Transformed*. New York: Macmillan, 1964.

Macpherson, C. B. *Democratic Theory: Essays in Retrieval*. London: Oxford University Press, 1973.

Martin, Roderick. "The Concept of Power: A Critical Defence." *The British Journal of Sociology*, 22, no. 3 (1971), pp. 240–256.

———. *The Sociology of Power*. London: Routledge & Kegan Paul, 1977.

May, Rollo. *Power and Innocence: A Search for the Sources of Violence*. New York: Norton, 1972.

Mechanic, David. "Sources of Power of Lower Participants in Complex Organizations." *Administrative Science Quarterly,* 7 (1962), pp. 349–364.

Merriam, Charles E. *Political Power*. New York: Collier Books, 1964.

Milgram, Stanley. *Obedience to Authority*. New York: Harper and Row, 1974.

Mill, John Stuart. *On Liberty*. New York: Appleton-Century-Crofts, 1947.

Mills, C. Wright. *The Power Elite*. New York: Oxford University Press, 1956.

Muller, Herbert J. *Issues of Freedom*. New York: Harper and Brothers, 1960.

Nagel, Jack H. *The Descriptive Analysis of Power*. New Haven: Yale University Press, 1975.

Nietzsche, Friedrich. *The Will to Power*. New York: Vintage Books, 1963.

Nyberg, David. "A Concept of Power for Education." *Teachers College Record,* 82 (1981), pp. 535–551.

———, ed. *The Philosophy of Open Education*. London: Routledge & Kegan Paul, 1975.

O'Brien, Conor Cruise and W. D. Vanech, eds. *Power and Consciousness*. New York: New York University Press, 1969.

Oliver, Donald W. and James P. Shaver. *Teaching Public Issues in the High School*. Boston: Houghton Mifflin, 1966.

Olsen, Marvine E., ed. *Power in Societies*. New York: Macmillan, 1970.

Oppenheim, Felix E. *Dimensions of Freedom*. New York: St. Martin's Press, 1961.

Parsons, Talcott. "The Distribution of Power in American Society." *World Politics,* 10, no. 1 (1957), pp. 123–143.

———. "On the Concept of Influence." *Political Opinion Quarterly,* 27 (1963), pp. 37–62, 87–92.

———. "On the Concept of Political Power." *Proceedings of the American Philosophical Society,* 107 (1963), pp. 232–262.

———. *Sociological Theory and Modern Society*. New York: Free Press, 1967.

Partridge, P. H. *Consent and Consensus*. New York: Praeger, 1971.

———. "Freedom." *The Encyclopedia of Philosophy*. Ed. Paul Edwards. New York: Macmillan, 1967, vol. 3, pp. 221–225.

——. "Some Notes on the Concept of Power." *Political Studies,* 11, no. 2 (1963), pp. 107-125.

Passigli, Stefano. "On Power, Its Intensity and Distribution." *European Journal of Political Research,* 1, no. 2 (1973), pp. 163-177.

Peters, R. S. *Ethics and Education.* London: Allen and Unwin, 1976.

Plato. *Gorgias, Republic.*

Potter, David M. *Freedom and Its Limitations in American Life.* Stanford: Stanford University Press, 1976.

Reid, Louis Arnauld. *Philosophy and Education.* New York: Random House, 1965.

Riker, W. H. "Some Ambiguities in the Notion of Power." *American Political Science Review,* 58 (1964), pp. 341-349.

Rogers, Carl R. *Freedom to Learn.* Columbus, Ohio: Charles E. Merrill, 1969.

——. *On Personal Power: Inner Strength and Its Revolutionary Impact.* New York: Delacorte, 1977.

Rogow, Arnold A. and Harold D. Lasswell. *Power, Corruption, and Rectitude.* Englewood Cliffs, N.J.: Prentice-Hall, 1963.

Rousseau, J. J. *Émile.* London: Everyman's Library, 1977.

Russell, Bertrand. *Power: A New Social Analysis.* New York: Norton, 1938.

Schattschneider, E. E. *The Semi-Sovereign People.* New York: Holt, Rinehart and Winston, 1960.

Seeman, M. "Powerlessness and Knowledge: A Comparative Study of Alienation and Learning." *Sociometry,* 30 (1967), pp. 105-123.

Singer, Benjamin D. "The Future-Focused Role-Image." *Learning for Tomorrow.* Ed. Alvin Toffler. New York: Vintage, 1974.

Skinner, B. F. *Beyond Freedom and Dignity.* New York: Knopf, 1971.

Spitz, David. "The Nature and Limits of Freedom." *Dissent,* 8 (Winter, 1961), pp. 78-85.

Thibaut, J. W. and H. H. Kelley. *The Social Psychology of Groups.* New York: Wiley, 1959.

Thucydides. *The Complete Writings of Thucydides: The Peloponnesian War.* New York: Modern Library, 1951.

Walter, E. V. "Power and Violence." *American Political Science Review,* 58, no. 2 (1964), pp. 350-360.

Weber, Max. *The Theory of Social and Economic Organization.* London: Oxford University Press, 1947.

Weiss, Paul. *Man's Freedom.* Carbondale and Edwardsville: Southern Illinois University Press, 1950.

Weizenbaum, Joseph. *Computer Power and Human Reason: From Judgment to Calculation.* San Francisco: W. H. Freeman, 1976.

White, D. M. "Power and Intention." *American Political Science Review*, 65, no. 3 (1971), pp. 749–759.

——. "The Problem of Power." *British Journal of Political Science, 2,* no. 4 (1972), pp. 479–490.

Wicklund, Robert A. *Freedom and Reactance.* New York: Wiley, 1974.

Wilson, John. "Two Types of Teaching." *Philosophical Analysis and Education.* Ed. R. D. Archambault. London: Routledge & Kegan Paul, 1965.

Wilson, John R. S. "In One Another's Power." *Ethics,* 88, no. 4 (1978), pp. 299–315.

Winter, David G. *The Power Motive.* New York: Free Press, 1973.

Wolfinger, Raymond E. "Nondecisions and the Study of Local Politics." *American Political Science Review,* 65, no. 4 (1971), pp. 1063–1104. (Includes a "Comment" by F. W. Frey, and Wolfinger's rejoinder.)

Woodhead, A. G. *Thucydides on the Nature of Power.* Cambridge: Harvard University Press, 1970.

Wrong, Dennis H. *Power: Its Forms, Bases, and Uses.* New York: Harper and Row, 1980.

——. "Some Problems in Defining Social Power." *American Journal of Sociology,* 76, no. 6 (1968), pp. 673–681.

Young, Michael F. D., ed. *Knowledge and Control.* London: Collier-Macmillan, 1971.

Zald, Mayer N., ed. *Power in Organizations.* Nashville: Vanderbilt University Press, 1970.

Zaleznik, A. and M. F. R. Kets de Vries. *Power and the Corporate Mind.* Boston: Houghton Mifflin, 1975.

Index

POWER OVER POWER

Designed by Richard E. Rosenbaum.
Composed by The Composing Room of Michigan, Inc.
in 10 point Century Schoolbook V.I.P., 2 points leaded,
with display lines in Century Schoolbook.
Printed offset by Thomson/Shore, Inc. on
Warren's Number 66 Antique Offset, 50 pound basis.
Bound by John H. Dekker & Sons, Inc.
in Holliston book cloth
and stamped in Kurz-Hastings foil.

Library of Congress Cataloging in Publication Data

Nyberg, David, 1943–
    Power over power.

    Bibliography: p.
    Includes index.
    1. Power (Social sciences) 2. Liberty. 3. Education—Philosophy.
I. Title.
HM271.N9   303.3'3   81-67053
ISBN 0-8014-1414-8   AACR2